Scene Scripts

Longman Imprint Books
General Editor: Michael Marland CBE

LONGMAN IMPRINT BOOKS

Scene Scripts

seven television plays
from the BBC School TV series, *Scene*
by

Michael Cahill
Keith Dewhurst
Rex Edwards
Ronald Eyre
Bill Lyons
Alan Plater
Fay Weldon

selected and edited by
Michael Marland BA
Headmaster, Woodberry Down School

with an article on producing plays for television by
Ronald Smedley
Senior Producer, BBC School Television

Longman

LONGMAN GROUP LIMITED
Longman House
Burnt Mill, Harlow, Essex

© *Editorial matter Longman Group Ltd 1972*
All rights reserved. No part of this publication may
be reproduced, stored in a retrieval system, or
transmitted in any form or by any means,
electronic, mechanical, photocopying, recording
or otherwise, without the prior permission of the
Copyright owner.

First published 1972
Seventh impression 1981

ISBN 0 582 23334 8

Printed in Hong Kong by
Sheck Wah Tong Printing Press Ltd

Contents

Acknowledgements

The editor and publisher are grateful to the following for permission to include scripts which are in copyright. Applications for performance rights should be addressed to the authors' agents:

Michael Cahill c/o Fraser and Dunlop (Scripts) Ltd,
91 Regent Street, London W.1.

Keith Dewhurst c/o Elspeth Cochrane Agency, 31A Sloane Street,
Knightsbridge, London S.W.1.

Rex Edwards c/o Harvey Unna Ltd, 14 Beaumont News, Marylebone High
Street, London W.1.

Ron Eyre c/o Hatton and Bradley Ltd, 17A Curzon Street, London W.1.

Bill Lyons c/o James Viccars Management Ltd, 179 Wardour Street,
London W.1.

Alan Plater c/o Margaret Ramsay Ltd, 14A Goodwin's Court,
St. Martin's Lane, London W.C.2.

Fay Weldon c/o Clive Goodwin Associates, 79 Cromwell Road, London, S.W.7.

They are also grateful to the BBC for permission to reproduce stills from plays they have produced, and also to the artistes concerned.

Clean Sweep: Jack Le White, Raymond Hunt, Barry Jackson, Brian Osborne
Terry: Dennis Waterman
£60 Single, £100 Return: Simon Ward, Margery Mason
Time Hurries On: Lucy Fleming, Alan Ross
Hero in the Dust: Michael Grady, Ralph Watson, Barry McCarthy, Tony Harrington, Charles Bolton
It's Me Eileen: Ann Salingar, Geraldine Sherman, Miriam Raymond, Ken Jones, Bill Lyons, Margaret Heald, Michael Wilsh
Last Bus: Paddy Joyce, Kenneth Gardnier, David Lincoln, Jane Carr, Noel Dyson, Will Leighton, Peter Delmar

Scene Scripts

For a start these are seven good stories. "Good" simply because they make most audiences interested in the people in them, what they are thinking and feeling, and what happens to them. Each of the plays was specially written for the BBC School Television series *Scene*. This is broadcast to schools, and a very large number of older pupils up and down the country have watched and enjoyed the plays.

But the series was trying to do more than put over good stories: the series was looking at some of the problems of life and the difficulties of the society we live in. Although each writer has invented characters and a situation which he finds personally fascinating, you will also find that each play is based on a difficulty. The characters get themselves out of the difficulty as best they can—but each play leaves us something to think over, to talk about—even to argue about.

As they were originally written for television, it is also interesting to use them as a starting point for discussion of *other* plays on television. The producer of them has described how he sets about his job on page 162. The scripts are effective read aloud in a classroom, and you will also find that they can be easily tape-recorded. If a group wants to stage one, they will find that most of them (perhaps not the last) can be easily acted on a simple stage. And the situations are good starting points for improvisations.

All the people in these plays are ordinary young people. The plays aren't deliberately made to be exciting or dramatic, but as you see each of these people facing the decisions in their lives, you will share their experiences. That's what makes an interesting play, after all.

MICHAEL MARLAND

"£60 Single, £100 Return"

by Bill Lyons

The Cast

Pete
Mrs Bray, *his widowed mother*
Des
Mr Potter
Mrs Potter   *his parents*
Jo, *his sister*

Pete and Des are two ordinary boys in a small town, working at reasonable jobs where they've been for a year and a half; they have few strong ambitions, but often seem dissatisfied with the place, their jobs, and their families. Des strikes one as the tougher, and it is he who finds the ad for a trip to India. Des persuades Pete to join him, though Pete seems tied to his widowed mother and far less adventuresome. But it's one thing talking a lot, and another actually seeing an idea through . . .

"£60 Single, £100 Return"

Evening in a small café

We see a close up of a fruit machine; then Pete reading a newspaper. An advert from the newspaper fills the screen before we cut to Pete again.

PETE You're joking, mate.

DES No I'm not. There I'll be, up on my elephant with some dolly bird in a sari.

PETE The Indian Restaurant at the top of our road is about as close as you'll get.

DES That's all you know, Pete. A touch of your Eastern promise—twanging away on my sitar I'll be.

PETE Some hopes!

DES Well it's a bit more exotic than your holiday camp chalets, mate.

PETE More expensive too. Hey, Des, about those chalets, Ginger Harris stayed in one last year and he reckoned it was pretty good.

DES Well, that's no recommendation, is it? If Ginger Harris and his screaming kids liked it, it can't be any good. You know what he said to me the other day. "Potter", he says, "if you're going to become a supervisor you'll have to buck your ideas up."

PETE You don't think he could stop them promoting you, do you?

DES It won't bother me if he does, mate.

PETE *(reading the advert again)* "India—£60 Single, £100 Return." That's a lot of money, Des.

DES I've got thirty pounds in the Post Office. I reckon we could raise the rest in two months.

PETE "Minibus leaves 6th July." You really thinking of going?

DES Of course. Why not?

PETE Well, supposing you could raise a hundred pounds, and I doubt that, you've got your job to think about. India isn't just round the corner you know. You'd be off work for weeks.

DES Oh, yeh. Well, that'd be no hardship.

PETE You'd get the sack. We've been there eighteen months now, Des.

DES You are not going to tell me that you've enjoyed it, are you?

PETE No, but it's still eighteen months work and when Tommy Barker gets made up, it's supervising for one of us, most like.

DES Big deal.

PETE Another three pounds ten a week.

DES There's plenty of better jobs around; another eighteen months and I can work my way up again. It's a chance to see somewhere, do something. My old man has never been further than Blackpool—except in the war—my mum certainly hasn't. Well, I'm going to be able to look back on something when I'm their age. You can have the supervising job and welcome to it.

PETE Anyway, you don't know anything about this advert. Girl in our road got into some dance troupe that was going to Turkey, and nobody has heard anything from her since.

DES That's birds. They're not likely to want me for anyone's harem now, are they?

PETE 'S'pose not. Can't imagine anyone fancying you. Look, if you want to get a hundred quid to go to India, you want to stop chucking your money down that thing.

DES It's due to come up, Pete! Look at all those tanners! The jackpot will go towards it.

Des plays the machine and loses again.

DES I know why you don't want to go anyway.

PETE Oh yeh?

DES It's not your job; it's your mum.

PETE Oh, shut up.

DES Yes, it is. Mummy would be upset. Who'd change your nappies? She'd have a fit if she thought her little Peter was going all those miles away.

PETE That's not like you, Des. Since dad died we've always gone on holiday together. Mum was dead choked when I told her I was going on holiday with you this year. How do you think she'd feel if I said I was going to India and chucking my job in as well?

Des plays the fruit machine, and shrugs.

PETE I can't ignore her. I've got to think how she'll feel about things.

DES Yeh.

PETE I would like to go though.

DES You would?

PETE We might be able to raise the money if we did a part time job as well. We've got our evenings and weekends free . . . .

DES O.K. Then let's go.

As the camera cuts, we hear the sound of a radio playing.

Pete's house that evening

In close up we see a woman's hands holding a photograph. Mrs Bray is tidying up after visitors. Everything is put back neatly in its place. She is dusting over a photo of the late Mr Bray and one of a baby. She finds a toy left by her visitor and puts it safely away. We hear the front door. She looks at her watch. Pete comes in.

MRS BRAY You're late tonight.

PETE Me and Des went out after work.

Mrs Bray expects a kiss. Pete gives her a dutiful peck on the cheek,

MRS BRAY You missed Doris, she brought little Howard over. Well, they waited as long as they could, but she had to get back to make Henry's dinner.

PETE I'm sorry. I didn't expect to be so long.

MRS BRAY I wouldn't have started cooking if I'd known you were going out with Des.

PETE I'll let you know another time.

MRS BRAY Well, I hope it hasn't spoiled. Little Howard really is growing up now; I wish you'd seen him.

Mrs Bray goes through to the kitchen. Pete picks up an apple out of the fruit bowl and munches into it. Mrs Bray returns with the meal.

MRS BRAY Oh, and I just said your meal was ready—you can't wait two minutes, can you?

PETE It's all going to the same place, isn't it?

MRS BRAY That's not the point, you should eat your meal first. Where did you go then, you and Des?

PETE Nowhere special.

MRS BRAY Oh yes, where's that?

PETE Down the caff.

MRS BRAY Chucking your money away down there again, were you?

PETE Just a couple of bob.

MRS BRAY That's the sort of thing you'll be doing on this holiday of yours and Des's, I suppose—losing your money in fruit machines.

PETE I doubt that.

MRS BRAY It really was a shame you missed them, Peter. They're not babies long, you know.

PETE Doris and Henry wanted you to go away with them last year, didn't they? Have they asked you this time?

MRS BRAY Hmmm.

The Potters' house, the same evening

Des is on the telephone in the hall. Through the door he can see his parents worshipping the television.

DES No, there'd be two of us coming—me and my mate . . . I suppose we'll have to fix up about passports and things quite soon, will we?
His sister, Jo, passes through the hall.

JO Have you seen my hairbrush?

DES I'm on the phone.

JO I can see that. Oh don't bother yourself.
She goes into the room.

DES Sorry about that. Look, how soon do we have to give you the hundred pounds?

Back in Pete's house

MRS BRAY India!

PETE   Well why not, I'm young—you've got to do things when you're young or you'll never do anything.

MRS BRAY   But what on earth would you want to go to India for?

PETE   (*patiently and firmly*) Mum I've never been anywhere, not been out of the country.

MRS BRAY   Well of course not; I've never had the money to take you abroad.

PETE   I didn't mean that.

MRS BRAY   I've had other things to spend money on.

PETE   I'd like to see something different—even if it's just once.

MRS BRAY   But do you have to go to India to see something different, you silly boy? And what's this advertisement? . . . do you know anything about these people. Is it a proper firm? Is it an organised holiday, or what?

PETE   I'm going to change my shirt.
Pete leaves the room.

MRS BRAY   (*calling after him*) And what about your job? You don't think about these things, do you? (*We can hear Pete moving about upstairs.*) Do you think they'd wait around while you go driving off to India? You were just in line for promotion too.

PETE   (*heard from upstairs*) Then I'd never be able to go.
There is a sound of drawers being opened

MRS BRAY   Top drawer; I ironed it this morning.

PETE   Mum, just once I want to do something.

MRS BRAY   Just once.
Pete returns.

MRS BRAY   It's because of Des. When he got his motorbike you were just the same.

PETE   Well, I didn't get one, did I?

MRS BRAY   It's a good thing too. Only the other day I was reading how many boys of your age have been killed riding those things.

PETE   Look, mum, it's just for this year, next year we'll have a great holiday together.

MRS BRAY   I'm not thinking about my holidays, Peter. I don't want you to worry about me.

PETE   But I do worry about you, mum, course I do.

The Potters' house again

Des puts the phone down with a flourish. He comes in from the hall but nobody takes any notice. He hums an Indian chant. Potter adjusts the volume on the TV wrestling. Des begins his version of an eastern dance. After this has taken him to standing on the edge of the sofa without any reaction, he sits.

DES Guess who's going to India then.

We see a close-up of Mr Potter's weak reaction.

DES (*repeats*) Guess who's going to India then.

POTTER Yer, what?

DES India. The exotic east.

JO Cup of tea before you go?

MRS P. You are a love, Jo. I was going to myself, but I want to see the end of this.

DES Your concern about me is really touching.

MRS P. What did you say, Des?

DES I'm thinking of going to India.

MRS P. Oh, yes.

DES For a sort of long holiday. I was on the phone about it.

POTTER You're always on that bloody phone about something; different if you paid for it.

JO I've put the kettle on, won't be long now. What's this about India, Des?

DES I'm going with Pete—minibus holiday to India. It was in the paper.

MRS P. Desmond, you're not serious.

DES Never been more serious in my life.

MRS P. You can't go to India.

DES See the world. Rolling stone and all that.

MRS P. How much does it cost, anyway?

DES Sixty pounds single, a hundred pounds return.

MRS P. Well, where would you get a hundred pounds from?

DES I'm going to save it up. I've got three months.

JO You, save a hundred pounds!

DES I saved for my bike.

MRS P. He did save for that, Jo.

JO Not a hundred pounds in three months, he didn't.

DES I've got thirty in the Post Office, and we're going to do a part time job as well.

JO Extra work—it'd kill you!

DES You'll be choked when you get your postcard from Delhi.

JO Amazed. (*Des begins to get up.*) Where are you off to now, China?

DES I am going to do some work on my bike. Can I have my tea in the yard, mum?
Des goes out to yard.

MRS P. You don't think he will?

POTTER Will what?

MRS P. Go to India.

POTTER What, him!
Kettle whistle is heard.

JO I'll do it.

POTTER Do something with that aerial, will you?
Jo prods the aerial and exits.

MRS P; Remember when he was going to become an ace reporter, all those letters he wrote after jobs—that all died down in a few weeks.

POTTER Yeh.

MRS P. Then he was going to take flying lessons, become a pilot. Never did that either, did he? He won't go to India.

POTTER No. Course he won't.

MRS P. He does get some mad ideas though. You have a talk with him. Just in case.

POTTER You know what kids are. If he thinks we don't want him to go, he really will be determined.
Jo comes in with the tea.

JO Here you are, Dad. Here's your tea.

POTTER While you're up, pass us my fags will you Jo?

MRS P I wish he wouldn't start this sort of thing, he knows it upsets me.
Jo passes the fags then carries two cups of tea out to the yard and bangs one down next to Des.

JO China or India?

DES Drop off.

JO   Never fancied going to India myself...

DES   No? Well I think it'll be great and the journey should be terrific too from what he was saying. I'm seeing the bloke that's organising it over the weekend and he's going to show me all the maps and everything.

JO   Fun for you! I couldn't do anything like that anyway. Even if I had the money, Mum and Dad would never let me go; they worry about me if I cross the road.

DES   Yeh, well, it's never the same for girls, is it?

JO   No, it's not fair.

She is examining the contents of the saddlebag, and finds a book.

Pete's house

Pete is on the phone.

PETE   Hullo, could I speak to Mr Bray please... Hullo, Uncle David, it's me—Peter... How's Auntie Elsie?... oh dear. Look, the reason why I rang, well, the thing is, I was wondering if you could use any help in the shop, part time you know, evenings or weekends? Could you, oh that'd be great. Can I start this Friday night? Only I want to be earning the extra as soon as possible...

Mrs Bray comes in followed by Des.

MRS BRAY   Who's that?

PETE   Nothing.

MRS BRAY   Someone to see you.

PETE   Won't be a minute, Des. Well, thanks again... see you Friday night.

Pete hangs up. Mrs Bray exits.

DES   Your mum has that way of always making me feel welcome.

PETE   Don't worry about her—she doesn't mean it. She likes you really.

DES   You could have fooled me.

PETE   She's not very keen on the India trip.

DES   That figures.

PETE   How did your lot take to the idea?

DES   Said I'd never raise the money—that was about all.

PETE   I've got myself a part time job.

DES   That was quick.

Pete hands Des a newspaper cutting.

PETE   Well I was going to apply for that, then I suddenly thought; remember when I was still at school and I used to help out at my uncle's shop.

DES   Yeh, you must have cost him a fortune the way you always got the change wrong.

PETE   Well I know he does late night shopping Fridays now, so I rang him up and asked if he could use me again. So now I'm doing Friday evening, all day Saturday, and Sunday morning.

DES   How much is he going to pay you then Pete?

PETE   Four pounds ten—not bad, is it?

DES   No, I wish I could find something. If I don't get some money from somewhere I won't be able to go.

PETE   Well what about that ad?

DES   Factory cleaning. That's for birds.

PETE   No it's not. Look, they're asking for fellers, so it must be special work, heavy or something. It works out at over four quid for three evenings a week.

DES   Not much of a job though, is it? I don't suppose your uncle . . . ?

PETE   Well, I'll ask him on Friday but I doubt if he will. I think he's only taking me on as a favour.

DES   No. Well never mind, I could do it I suppose.

PETE   I'll go and make us a cup of tea.

DES   Might not be too bad.

PETE   It's only for a few weeks.

DES   Yeh.

Mrs Bray comes into kitchen with a pile of washing.

PETE   I was just going to make a cup of tea.

MRS BRAY   You only had to ask, I'd have done it.

The yard of the Potters' house one evening

Des is working on his bike again. Jo enters.

JO   Hello, and how is Mrs Mop?

DES Another comedian.

JO Never thought of you as a char before. I bet your hands aren't all baby soft now.

DES It's not like being a char anyway. It is hard, that factory cleaning. Do you know, every bone in my body is aching. I kept looking up at the clock. I thought eleven would never come.

JO That clock must have been fast. It's only five to now, or is it 'cos your bike travels faster than time.

DES Get lost. They let me off early because I'm such a quick worker.

JO Oh yeh, you'll get the sack you know Des if you keep knocking off early. Remember what happened at Butlers.

DES Well that was the foreman, wasn't it? He had it in for me from the first day, that fella.

JO You won't be able to save up the money to go to India then, will you?

DES Stroll on.

JO I don't care; it doesn't matter to me if you go or not. Look, it's late. Des, don't you think you ought to leave that thing alone and let us all get some sleep?

DES I've nearly finished now.

Inside the Potters' house

Jo, Pete, and Des are sitting at the table with a large map in front of them. They drink coffee.

PETE And we'll be driving in down here.

DES Not long now and we'll be leaving.

PETE Yes. It seemed closer when we gave in the deposit, didn't it?

JO If something happens and you can't go . . . can you get the deposit back?

DES I don't know. It's like a pledge of good faith ain't it—he'd be entitled to hang on to it if you suddenly decided you didn't want to go.

PETE He might give it back—he's a nice bloke, but we're both going anyway. Look, Des, I better be going home. I said to Mum that I wouldn't be too late.

JO   Have another cup of coffee before you go.

PETE   No, I don't want to be too late.

DES   All right then—see you.

JO   Tara.

PETE   Bye. Goodbye, Mrs Potter, Mr Potter.

MRS P. Goodbye, Peter.
        Pete exits.

JO   I might go next year you know.

MRS P. What, to India?

JO   Well, why not?

MRS P. You couldn't go to India. I mean, well it's not a nice place
        for a young girl.

JO   What's wrong with it?

MRS P. Well, it's not . . . it's . . . it's not hygienic for a start.

DES   Oh I see, it's all right for me to get typhoid, but not Jo,
        thank you very much.

MRS P. That's not what I mean.

DES   Well, what do you mean?

MRS P. Their customs are different.

JO   What, you think they are going to arrest me for smuggling?

MRS P. Not those sort of customs. Their habits, you know—I
        mean they think it's all right to have three wives and that
        sort of thing.

DES   She couldn't find anyone to marry her, not even in
        India.

JO   Charming!

MRS P. Stan, you talk to her, she says she's going to India now.

POTTER No she's not, no more than Des is from what I've heard.

DES   What are you on about?

POTTER I was in the pub last night.

DES   That's not news.

POTTER Mate of mine told me that you'd lost that evening job in
        the factory. Late once too often, he said. Same old story,
        just like that other job he lost.

MRS P. Is this true, Des?

DES   Well . . .

JO   So you haven't got the money to go.

DES   I'll raise it somehow.

POTTER There is one way you could.

DES Oh, yeh?

POTTER Yeh. You could sell that bloody Jumbo jet out in the yard there, and then maybe we'll all get some peace.

DES What, my bike—after all the work I've put in on it.

POTTER It's the only way you'll raise the money in the time. So it depends how much you want to go, doesn't it?

DES All right then! If I have to. . . . If it's the only way, I will. If it's the only way.

Des goes out into the yard.

MRS P. You didn't mean that, did you, Stan?

POTTER Yes, why? Do him good to get rid of that thing.

MRS P. I mean he loves that bike like it was human—maybe he still won't have enough. How much will he get for it?

POTTER Fifty, maybe sixty, I suppose.

MRS P. That's more than he paid for it.

POTTER With all the work Des has put in on it it's worth more.

MRS P. Well, I don't think you ought to have told him to sell it.

POTTER Why?

MRS P. You don't want him miles away in India, do you?

POTTER Why not? He's not a child any more, love.

MRS P. You don't want to stop him?

POTTER Why should I? Anything that'll get rid of that bloody bike.

MRS P. Oh, Dad.

Jo looks up from her "true romance".

JO Well I think that Mum is right. You shouldn't let him sell it.

She goes out to yard.

POTTER Who'd have kids!

MRS P. You ought to do something about it. It's about time you put your foot down and told him to forget the whole thing. I don't think you care if he goes to India or not.

POTTER Well I do . . . it's just . . .

MRS P. Well stop him then, stop him selling that bike. Where are you going now?

Down the pub!

Potter exits, slamming the door.

Pete's house

Pete is reading while his mother sews. There is a heavy silence over the room.

MRS BRAY Since you're not going to be here much longer you might at least talk to me now.

PETE Sorry, mum—it's just that there's a bit about the match in here.

MRS BRAY Well, if that's more important . . .

PETE What was it that you wanted to talk about?

MRS BRAY Well, what do you think I want to talk to you about?

PETE Mum, let's not go on about it again.

MRS BRAY Well, I'm sorry if I go on about it. It's not really surprising though, is it? I am your mother; it would be a bit strange if I wasn't concerned about you going off to India with people I don't even know.

PETE You know Des.

MRS BRAY Oh yes, I know Des and I know you. You two off in India for no one knows how long. It's not surprising I'm worried sick, is it?

PETE Mum, we can look after ourselves.

MRS BRAY You don't think about me, do you, sitting here wondering if you'll ever come back.

PETE It's only a holiday, mum.

MRS BRAY Well it won't be a holiday for me. I don't suppose I'll sleep all the time you're away.

PETE Mum, it's just once in my life I want to do something that'll really be worth remembering.

MRS BRAY Maybe I'd have liked to have done something. Maybe I wanted something worth remembering. But we can't always do the things we want to do. (*We see a close up of Pete as she talks.*) I mean, I've had to spend my time looking after you, and it's not been easy, and now you've got your job, your future to think about and you're throwing it away. Do you really think you're going to come back and walk into another job that's as good as this one, just like that? No, Peter, I don't really want you to go.

PETE Mum, I've already told Des I'm going. I can't let him down now, can I?

MRS BRAY You can let me down—you can let yourself down. You'll just have to make up your mind which is more important—yourself, your mother, or this trip to India.
They look at each other.

PETE I feel like a walk.
Pete exits. We close on Mrs Bray.

The yard of the Potters' house

Des is working on his bike. Jo enters.

JO Dad says you've sold the bike. It's not true, is it?

DES Yeh.

JO What's it doing here then?

DES Well it's not quite definite as yet, but it's as good as. He's going to phone tonight to confirm.

JO Who's the lucky buyer, anyone I know?

DES Ginger Harris from work; you know he's always fancied my bike.

JO (*surprised*) Ginger Harris?

DES Yeh, thought I'd give him first chance.

JO How much is he going to pay for it?

DES I thought about fifty, seeing as how he's a mate. It's worth more.

JO Joan Harris'll never let him have fifty quid for a bike.

DES That's all you know; he's the boss in his own home.

JO Well, maybe but I doubt it.

DES No, it's practically definite, Jo. I said he's phoning tonight to confirm.
Pete comes out into yard to join them.

PETE Your mum said you were out here working on the bike.

DES Hello, mate. Wasn't expecting you.

PETE I wanted to go out for a walk and I thought, well I might just as well come over here . . . you know.

JO There's nothing wrong, is there?

PETE Well no . . . nothing that can't be sorted out I suppose.

DES Your mum's been giving you trouble again, has she Pete? I don't know why she's always going on at you, I mean you . . .

16

PETE (*interrupting*) It's not her fault. I understand how she feels.

DES Well, she is your mum, but . . . like I was saying, you are old enough to look after yourself.

PETE Leave it, Des. I see you haven't sold the bike yet—leaving it a bit late, aren't you?

DES Yeh, it is sold—gets collected in the morning. You'll never guess who's buying it. Ginger Harris from work.

PETE That's good anyway.

JO Dad'll be pleased.

Mrs Potter puts head round door.

MRS P. Phone call for you Des.

DES Coming.

MRS P. It's that Ginger Harris.

DES See. I told yer!

Des goes quickly into the house.

MRS P. What do you think, Jo? Joan Harris is expecting another baby.

JO When?

MRS P. She's five months gone.

JO Well, do you know I saw her when I took things to the launderette on Thursday and I thought that she'd put on a bit of weight, but I never realised she was pregnant.

MRS P. I can usually tell from the eyes.

JO What does she want, boy or girl?

MRS P. Well, Ginger didn't say but I should think they'd want a girl with two boys already. Wouldn't you, Peter?

PETE Yes. I suppose so.

MRS P. We'd better get back inside and get your Dad his supper.

Mrs Potter exits. Jo goes and sits on the motorbike.

JO Won't seem the same without this thing deafening us and stinking the place out.

PETE What, Des or the motorbike? (*Jo reacts.*) It's a good bike that.

JO You ought to get one.

PETE Well . . . not just at the moment.

Des comes back into the yard.

DES You won't believe what's happened.

17

JO   What's up, Des?

DES   That was Ginger Harris on the phone.

JO   Yeh, mum told us. Joan Harris is expecting again.

DES   I'm not bothered about that. Ginger has let me down.

JO   I didn't think he'd buy it, especially not with Joan pregnant again.

DES   Ginger Harris has let me down. I mean he's dropped me right in it.

JO   I think I'll go and see if mum needs any help with the supper.

Jo goes back into the house.

DES   I was letting him have it cheap too, cos I thought he was a mate.

PETE   I thought he'd already bought it.

DES   Well he'd as good as promised, and now he phones up and says that money is going to be a bit tighter with the new baby coming and anyway it would be more practical to save for a car.

PETE   Well, I suppose it would be.

DES   Well what about me? He said he was going to buy it. I needed that money to go to India. What am I going to do now?

PETE   You'll just have to find somebody else to buy it.

DES   There's no time Pete. I mean I know somebody in the trade and he was telling me that the bottom has dropped right out of the market. Sometimes takes them months to shift a secondhand bike. And I really wanted to go to India Pete, you know that. After all that work.

PETE   So you're giving the idea up?

DES   Oh no, I'm not giving it up. I'll go next year. Yeh, now that'd be best—we could go next year. We'll get the deposit back . . . sure to. I mean we tried to do it in a bit of a rush this year didn't we. We never really had enough time, but if we aimed for next year we'd be able to save up easy and have plenty of spending money and everything. Maybe it's best this way—we could probably still get into those chalets you were on about. I've got enough for that and you said that they were pretty good, didn't you? Shame

18

about Ginger letting us down but that's the way it goes. Wasn't my fault, was it?

PETE No.

DES Well I'll fix up about the chalets then, shall I? I bet they'll be pleased at work, wouldn't want to lose us, would they?

PETE Des, I've made up my mind. I'm going to India, not next year, not the year after that. On the sixth of July, like we said. And if you're not coming, Des, I'll go on my own.

We see a close up of the baffled face of Des, and then the determined face of Pete, before an Indian cave fills the screen, and the final captions come up.

Note. There is a description on p. 162 by the BBC producer of the way in which this play was produced.

Terry

by Alan Plater

The Cast

Terry, *about seventeen*
Janie, *his girl friend*
The Manager *of the factory where he works*
Terry's Mum
Terry's Dad
Maitland, *the Youth Employment Officer*
A clerk
Dave, *one of his friends*

Everyone, or almost everyone, has to have a job. For many there's not really much choice, but rather surprisingly most people nevertheless settle into a job with a fair amount of satisfaction, even pride. For the lucky ones there's real interest, and a feeling of getting somewhere: for others, though, there seems little point. Terry is one of those. Everything bores him—but is that his fault or that of the job? Nobody can help him, but is that his fault or theirs?

TERRY Well . . . (*He shrugs vaguely.*) . . . I don't like the uniform.

DAD When I was your age it was a khaki uniform . . . I was fighting for my country . . .

TERRY Home guard.

DAD We was ready; they'd only to set foot on our shores . . .

MUM Anyhow, at least it'd smarten you up a bit, our Terry.

TERRY I *am* smart. (*And he is, in his own way.*) You ask Janie.

The coffee bar at night

As we see Janie, Terry's voice can still be heard.

TERRY Janie, that's my bird. Sort of girl next door, except she lives three flaming miles away . . . long way on a wet night. But she's all right. (*Terry walks into the camera shot in the foreground.*) If you like that sort of thing. (*He crosses to the table and sits down with her. Jukebox playing—sort of discotheque music.*) You're all right really, aren't you love?

JANIE You're daft.

TERRY But I'm happy with it.

JANIE And unemployed.

TERRY Give us a kiss.

JANIE Shuttup! No wonder your mam and dad go spare . . .

TERRY Well, they've had theirs, haven't they?

JANIE I mean, what you trying to prove?

TERRY I mean, I don't want to spend the rest of my life putting cardboard boxes inside of other cardboard boxes.

JANIE Somebody's got to do it.

TERRY Same as road-sweeping and I'm not doing that, neither . . .

JANIE But you'll let other people do it, won't you?

TERRY I'll stand all day watching them. I love work; I can watch it for hours. . . .

JANIE I'm not joking, Terry.

TERRY Give us a kiss.

JANIE I said I'm not joking.

TERRY Neither am I.

JANIE How many jobs is this?

TERRY Depends when you're counting from.

JANIE Oh, I don't know . . . since Christmas . . .

27

TERRY   Can't even remember Christmas ... was it good? Did you give me a present?

JANIE   You're daft.

TERRY   Was it merry? Eh? Give us a kiss, pretend it's mistletoe time ...

JANIE   When you going to grow up?

TERRY   I'm not if I can help it.

JANIE   You're a fool to yourself (*But she kisses him. He looks over her shoulder into camera.*)

TERRY   Sometimes she sounds just like my mam.
Cut to:

The youth employment office

Mr Maitland is at work. He is in his thirties, quiet and conscientious. He has a kind of dedication and care in his attitude to his work, tempered by the realisation of the impossibilities of the job.

MAITLAND   Come in.
Terry comes in.

TERRY   Morning, Mr Maitland. (*To camera.*) Mr Maitland's the youth employment officer. He'll fix me up, no trouble ... well, he always has done before ...

MAITLAND   You want me to fix you up again ...

TERRY   Well, you always have done before.

MAITLAND   Reach into a magic top hat and produce an easy, healthy job at about thirty pounds a week, no special skill required.

TERRY   Just what I'm looking for.

MAITLAND   Me too.

TERRY   Oh ... thought you were serious.

MAITLAND   So you didn't get on very well with the cardboard boxes?

TERRY   I was going mad ... honest.

MAITLAND   Medical certificate?

TERRY   You what?

MAITLAND   Didn't you go to your doctor?

TERRY   You can't go to the doctor and say you're going mad ...

everybody would say you're balmy. (*Pause.*) No, what it was—it got so's I was trying to put the big boxes in the little ones . . . well, it's not on, is it? . . . you can't go on like that.

MAITLAND Some of us have to keep trying. Oh well, let's see . . . (*He checks through his files.*) Do you know the score so far?

TERRY What score?

MAITLAND Do you know how many jobs you've had since you left school?

TERRY Not exactly, no . . . I know it's a few . . .

MAITLAND Twenty-three jobs in just over two years.

TERRY Getaway! That's not bad is it?

MAITLAND Are you trying for a record?

TERRY Not really.

MAITLAND Good.

TERRY Mind you, if I'm anywhere near the record, I don't mind having a go . . .

MAITLAND We're not interested in breaking records, Terry . . .

TERRY O.K.

MAITLAND We just want the right people in the right jobs.

TERRY You're dead right there, Mr Maitland. There's too many people bothering about breaking records and that . . . instead of just being happy. Being happy, that's what counts, isn't it?

MAITLAND (*very patiently.*) Yes, that's what counts.

TERRY Yes.

MAITLAND Now . . . you didn't get any O levels, did you?

TERRY They didn't have any at our school . . .

MAITLAND I think they did.

TERRY Well, likely they did, but I didn't enter.

MAITLAND I see.

TERRY I'd only have failed so I didn't bother.

MAITLAND And you decided against an apprenticeship.

TERRY Well, you can't tell how you'll like it, can you? It's all for tomorrow . . .

MAITLAND How do you mean, all for tomorrow?

TERRY I was saying to my Dad, say you spend ten years learning to be a brain surgeon . . . and halfway through your first job, you find out you hate it ... well, you're in dead lumber, aren't you? So why bother?

MAITLAND We usually find you something in unskilled manual.

TERRY Well, I haven't got any skills and I'm sort of a man ... (*He laughs.*)

MAITLAND Manual doesn't mean that, Terry ...

TERRY I know, I'm having you on ... manual. Once a year. *Maitland reacts. He's used to it but ...*

MAITLAND Would you like to try something clerical?

TERRY Like a white collar job?

MAITLAND Yes.

TERRY I thought I was too thick for anything like that.

MAITLAND I haven't said you're thick, Terry ...

TERRY Because of the O levels ...

MAITLAND You can read and write ...

TERRY Yes.

MAITLAND And add up?

TERRY Long as they're not all at the same time.

MAITLAND Perhaps it'll be twenty-fourth time lucky.

TERRY (*turning to camera*) And that's how I become a business executive. (*He gets up and walks across to another door marked "Clerks" Department.*) I said to myself ... there's going to be some changes made.

Inside the Clerks' Department

Terry enters. He is now in approved white collar uniform—suit and white shirt and tie—in contrast to the smart but casual clothes he's been wearing up to this point.

TERRY Well, you've got to dress the part if you're an executive. I'm not kidding, I feel a right fairy in this rig, like I was off to my grandad's funeral. Here we go then.... (*He sits at desk.*) This is what you call a white collar job. Clean and respectable. I sit here, minding my own business, reading the paper or having a smoke, or both, and every now and then this happens ... (*A load of papers is thrown on-to the desk from out of sight.*) What we in the trade call a load of bumf. There's a lot of green bits of paper ... like these . . . and they've all got like sums of money written on . . . like three pounds fifteen and a tanner . . . or fifteen pounds nine shillings . . . or, here's a nice one . . . seven pounds, seven shillings and sevenpence halfpenny. (*He explains the job, doing it as he talks.*) I write all the numbers off the green bits of paper onto pink bits of paper, till the pink bit's full . . . like a list . . . and then I add it all up . . . (*He puts all the green bits on a spike when he's finished with them. He now ploughs agonisingly through the arithmetic.*) Now then . . . what's seventeen and fifteen and twenty-three and six and three and thirty-five . . . come on . . . quick, quick . . . carry seven and take away nine and . . . Oh, hell! (*Pause.*) Not easy, being an executive. Any road, I'm just explaining the principle of the thing . . . now, when I've added them all up on the pink bits of paper, a man called Ernest Armitage comes round . . . He's an office boy—about a hundred and seventy years old . . . He takes all the pink bits of paper away . . . don't ask me what it's all for, ask the International Moneybox Corporation . . . but I think this is what happens. They take the pink papers to another office and add them all up onto brown bits of paper . . . and then somebody writes those answers onto striped paper . . . and somebody else writes those answers onto sticks of rhubarb. And somebody else writes those answers on railway station walls . . . and somebody else writes those answers on the backs of five pound notes . . . (*Pause.*) And at tea time the buzzer goes and they get all the green paper, and pink paper, and brown paper, and striped paper, and rhubarb and station walls and five pound notes and burn the lot in the boilerhouse . . . till you get a nice pillar of smoke going up into the sky. Then they start all over again in the morning.

We cut to the Chief of Clerks.

CLERK You say the work's getting you down?

TERRY Yes, Mr Fankenheimer.

CLERK You think a rest would do you good?

TERRY I think it would be in the interests of the firm, Mr Fankenheimer.

31

The clerk looks at Terry's work which is lying on the desk.

CLERK I'm sure it would. (*He gives Terry his cards.*) I'm sure it would.
We move into a close shot of the clerk's face—in which anxiety is mixed with temporary relief.

The coffee bar at night

JANIE You're daft.

TERRY You keep on saying that.

JANIE You keep on being daft.

TERRY All them numbers . . . my brain, it wouldn't keep still . . .

JANIE If you'd stuck at it . . . practice makes perfect.

TERRY The more I did it, the worse I was at it.

JANIE You can't have been very interested.

TERRY You're dead right there, I wasn't interested . . . I mean, they never told you what it was about . . . all those sums of money . . . you couldn't tell what they were for . . . you never saw the money.
They are joined by Dave, Terry's mate. He is brash, self-confident—about the same age as Terry.

DAVE Who mentioned money?

TERRY I thought you'd hear that.

DAVE Haven't got an alarm clock at home . . . just a tape recording of somebody dropping half a dollar on the floor . . .

TERRY (*Direct to the camera*) This is Dave . . . my mate . . . he's a proper nutcase, but you can't help liking him.

DAVE Are you coming down the bowling alley?

TERRY No.

DAVE What's up? Scared of losing?

TERRY Can't afford it.

JANIE He's out of work again.

TERRY I'm only resting.

JANIE That's a new word for it.

DAVE Are you coming, Janie?

JANIE Why should I?

DAVE I got the money.

TERRY You're not working are you?

DAVE   Sort of casual. When I feel like it ... and this horse won at six to one ...

TERRY   So what are you doing?

DAVE   I'm spending it, you nit. (*To Janie*) Are you coming, love?

JANIE   No, I'm stopping here with him.

DAVIE   You want your brains washing. See you.

    Dave goes out.

JANIE   He's right.

TERRY   What?

JANIE   I do want my brains washing.

TERRY   Don't take any notice of Dave.

JANIE   But when are you going to pull yourself together, Terry?

TERRY   When I start falling apart. (*To the camera*) Sometimes she sounds *very* like my mam.

Terry's living room at night

MUM   I wish he'd pull himself together.

DAD   No chance.

MUM   Did you have a word with Tommy?

DAD   Tommy who?

MUM   Tommy Hodgkinson.

DAD   Oh, aye.

MUM   What's he say?

DAD   Send Terry along, he'll have a word with him.

MUM   Good.

DAD   No promises, mind ...

MUM   But he owes you a favour, does Tommy Hodgkinson.

DAD   Why does he?

MUM   You give him them tomato plants, didn't you?

DAD   Yes, I did that.

MUM   Well then ...

DAD   They all died.

MUM   But the thought was there.

DAD   Happen so. Anyhow, he says he'll see Terry.

MUM   That's grand. (*There is a pause.*) Have you mentioned it to him?

DAD To Terry? Yes.

MUM What did he say?

The coffee bar

The screen is filled with a big close up of Terry.

TERRY Get lost! (*Cutting to a two-shot of Janie and Terry as he goes on.*) Well, who wants to work for British rotten Railways ...? Swilling down the platforms, and picking up wastepaper and carrying bags for people that's too fat and lazy to do it for themselves ...

JANIE It's not as bad as that.

TERRY No, it's the uniform ... really, well, you look like a German soldier in an old war picture! You can keep all that ...

JANIE There isn't a job in the whole world to suit you.

TERRY There should be something, somewhere ...

JANIE You've had every job there is and you haven't found it yet!

TERRY No, I'll just have to keep on trying till I get the one I want.

JANIE That'll be never.

TERRY You can't tell. (*The record changes on the jukebox and so does Terry's mood.*) Did I tell you, once on holiday, Scarborough it was, I found a bit of wood on the beach.

JANIE No, you didn't tell me.

TERRY I thought I did.

JANIE (*mocking*) Terry found a bit of wood on the beach at Scarborough, read all about it ...

TERRY Sort of driftwood, I suppose ... well it was a bit of wood and it had drifted in on the tide so that makes it driftwood, doesn't it? Wood that drifts.

JANIE (*sarcastically*) Brilliant!

TERRY So I whittled it.

JANIE You what?

TERRY Whittled it ... with a knife ... All week, didn't bother with dodgems and fruit machines and that, I just whittled at this bit of wood . . . I still had some money left, end of the week. . . .

JANIE   Fancy

TERRY   I whittled this . . . like . . .

JANIE   What?

TERRY   Well, some ways you looked at it, it was like a horse . . . and other ways it wasn't . . .

JANIE   (*dismissing him*) I always said you was daft.

TERRY   Remember at school, we had that trip, round that old church, no not a church, bigger than that . . .

JANIE   It was a minster.

TERRY   There was some there do you remember?

JANIE   What? Fellers whittling?

TERRY   Don't be filthy.

JANIE   You said . . .

TERRY   No . . . like carvings out of wood . . . on the ends of all the seats.

JANIE   The pews . . . pews in a church.

TERRY   Well, then . . .
        (*There is a pause.*)

JANIE   Well then what?

TERRY   That's what I'd like to do . . . the feller that carves the . . . the carvings on the end of the . . .

JANIE   The ends of the seats . . .

TERRY   The ends of the pews . . . in churches and minsters . . . that's what I'd like to be . . .

JANIE   Well, you can't, 'cause they don't build them any more.

TERRY   They build churches.

JANIE   Not big ones, and they don't have carvings on the ends anyway . . . it's all plastic and bent metal.

TERRY   Makes no odds. That's what I'd like to be.

JANIE   Like everything. It's all plastic and bent metal, everywhere you look.

TERRY   I don't care. (*He pauses, and then is more certain.*) That's what I want to be.

JANIE   (*to the camera*) He wants locking up.

Terry's living room

MUM I've just lost patience with him.

DAD I could hit him.

The youth employment office

MAITLAND (*Speaking into the camera*) Some days . . . I just can't explain it but it's like second sight . . . somebody knocks at the door and I know it's going to be *him*. (*louder*) Come in . . . (*Terry comes in.*) . . . Terry. (*Terry sits down.*) Back again?

TERRY Yes. Time to exchange my labour again.

MAITLAND I don't know what we're going to do this time . . .

TERRY (*to the camera*) He looks a bit worried . . . overwork, I should think.

MAITLAND The International Moneybox Corporation seem to think clerical work isn't for you.

TERRY I agree with them there . . .

MAITLAND That's something.

TERRY They had some numbers I'd never head of before.

MAITLAND They said your arithmetic showed more imagination than accuracy.

TERRY I'm too thick to understand that, not having my O-levels.

MAITLAND How is your arithmetic?

TERRY Improving . . . I've got some new tablets.

MAITLAND Terry!

TERRY What's the matter?
There is a pause. Maitland takes a deep breath.

MAITLAND What's 58 from 73?

TERRY Just over twenty.

MAITLAND Approximately?

TERRY Oh yes, it's only approximate.

MAITLAND And if I put five bob on a horse that wins at a hundred to eight, how much have I to come?

TERRY (*After only a brief pause.*) Three pounds, two and six, plus your stake money and less tax.

MAITLAND Approximately?

TERRY	To the penny.
MAITLAND	That was quick.
TERRY	Well, that's useful, isn't it?
MAITLAND	I suppose so. (*Pause.*) You're a problem aren't you, Terry?
TERRY	I'm not, am I?
MAITLAND	If I send you along to an employer, he wants to know what previous experience you've had.
TERRY	I've had stacks of experience . . .
MAITLAND	I know but . . .
TERRY	There's not many kids of my age had as much experience as me. It's an advantage, isn't it?
MAITLAND	But an employer prefers it if you're going to stay for a reasonable length of time . . .
TERRY	That's up to him.
MAITLAND	In what way is it up to him?
TERRY	He's running the thing.
MAITLAND	So . . . ?
TERRY	Well, if he doesn't like me not sticking at the job, he can always sack me . . .
MAITLAND	What if you're leaving anyway?
TERRY	It's up to him to get in first . . .
MAITLAND	Doesn't solve anything.
TERRY	Proves who's boss.
MAITLAND	You've lost me, Terry.
TERRY	I'm sorry. Should I say it again?
MAITLAND	No, let's leave it for now . . .
TERRY	Please yourself. It's all to do with machines though.
MAITLAND	Machines?
TERRY	That's the trouble. Say there's this factory full of machines . . . nothing very fancy, just a lever and a handle, say . . . and the man pays me ten quid a week to work the handle . . . right? . . . well, that makes me part of the machine . . .
MAITLAND	In a way.
TERRY	Well I don't mind pretending I'm a machine, if he's paying me to pretend. But if I suddenly decide I'd rather be a feller . . . not a machine, just a human being . . . that's it, isn't it? I've got to sling my hook, haven't I?

MAITLAND   A lot of people don't.

TERRY   That's up to them. (*He pauses.*) Is that what you go to school for?

MAITLAND   What?

TERRY   To learn how to be a machine without moaning about it?

MAITLAND   I wouldn't say so.

TERRY   Well if it isn't that, it must be to learn how to be a human being . . . but you can't have both, can you?

MAITLAND   (*Pause.*) It's not my job to answer questions about the education system.

TERRY   But everybody's in it, aren't they? You, me, my dad, teachers, my mates . . . machines is it? Or people is it? I don't know, I wish somebody'd tell me . . . but I'll tell you this for nothing . . . you can't have both . . . not in the same feller. You can't have both.

MAITLAND   What sort of job had you in mind, Terry?

TERRY   (*reverting coldly to business*) What have you got in?

MAITLAND   Not very much.

TERRY   Can you fix me up with a job whittling pew ends?

MAITLAND   (*After a pause.*) Whittling pew ends?

TERRY   In like cathedrals or minsters . . . ordinary churches even, if you've got nothing else.

(*Maitland goes through the motions of checking the filing cards.*)

MAITLAND   There seems to be nothing under whittling.

TERRY   Pity about that . . . I really fancy whittling pew ends.

MAITLAND   You'll have to come again next week.

TERRY   (*Loudly and harshly into the camera*) Can you come back next week?

The coffee bar

Janie and Terry.

JANIE   (*in close-up*) He said that last week.

TERRY   I know.

JANIE   And the week before.

TERRY   And the week before that.

JANIE   So what are you going to do?

TERRY   Going back next week.

38

JANIE	You're just messing about.
TERRY	I'm not messing about! He's the one that's messing about. If he hasn't got any whittling jobs in, that's not my fault.
JANIE	He's got *some* jobs in, hasn't he?
TERRY	If you can call them that.
JANIE	Beggars can't be choosers.
TERRY	Begging, I hadn't thought of that . . .
JANIE	You're a fool.
TERRY	With sandwich boards on, something like that, no that's not begging, is it? All right though, I might ask him about that.
JANIE	You're a layabout, Terry.
TERRY	No, I'm not!
JANIE	You're no sort of a feller if you can't get yourself a job and stand on your own feet.
TERRY	I see. That's what you think, is it?
JANIE	That's what I think. And not just that.
TERRY	You're thinking something else? Two things at once, that's very good for you.
JANIE	Get yourself sorted out good and quick . . . or else get yourself another girl friend . . .
TERRY	I don't want two girl friends.
JANIE	Terry . . . (*She catches his attention, and pauses.*) You can find somebody else to take out.
TERRY	I see.
JANIE	I'm fed up of paying anyway.
TERRY	Right then. (*To the camera*) They're all closing in on me now.

The living room

MUM	Terry.
TERRY	What?
MUM	Has your Dad spoken to you?
TERRY	Not for about six weeks.
MUM	I'll tell you myself . . .
TERRY	Is it birds and bees? We had that at school . . .
MUM	He's made an appointment for you.

TERRY I had it cut last week.

MUM To see Tommy Hodgkinson.

TERRY You what?

MUM Four o'clock on Friday.

TERRY Tommy who?

MUM Hodgkinson . . . your Dad's foreman.

TERRY King of the railroad.

MUM So you'd better go.

TERRY (*after a pause*) Mam . . .

MUM Yes, Terry . . .

TERRY Supposing . . . just supposing I don't turn up . . .
We see that Dad has come back, and is standing in the doorway.

DAD You can find yourself some fresh parents.

TERRY (*To the camera*) It's a game isn't it? (*Then, with a change of expression.*) No, it isn't.
Terry sets off on a tour of his situation. He walks us round the studio, pausing to observe or converse with the people in his life. They are all in their established settings, as we have seen them so far.

TERRY (*Looking at his mother and father, in their sitting room*) Parents, well, you can't blame them I suppose . . . they deserve better treatment than I can give them.

MUM I just want him to be happy that's all.

DAD That's right.

MUM That's all anybody wants.

TERRY That's all I want, mother dear, to be happy . . . but it's easier said than done, and I'm sure it's not knitting and football pools and Coronation Street . . . (*He walks into a two-shot with Janie.*) And love's young dream. Yes, she's dreaming . . . the little house, and the fitted carpet and the dog called Spot . . . and you can't have that if you're married to a waster like Terry . . .

JANIE I'm not unreasonable, it's just what any normal girl wants.

TERRY True.

JANIE (*Trying to persuade us*) And it's not just for me, it's for his sake . . . I want him to be happy . . .

TERRY   There you are again, happy ... I know all about the little house and the rest of it. She thinks I don't listen but I take it all in. I know when she stops outside a shop window ...

JANIE   He could be happy if only he'd let himself.

TERRY   But happy's whittling wood isn't it? Nobody's going to let me do that, are they? It's all either numbers or boxes ... and they don't even tell you what it's for ... nobody can explain.

He walks close to Maitland, who is at his desk.

MAITLAND   Well, I won't pretend Terry's my easiest customer.

TERRY   You can say that again.

MAITLAND   I won't pretend Terry's my ...

TERRY   (*breaking in*) It's a joke.

MAITLAND   But I've a sneaking suspicion he'll settle down in time; they usually do.

TERRY   Get yourself a wife and three kids, you've no option. But that's not settling down,—that's blackmail. You've got to join the machine then ...

He walks into a two-shot with Hackenschmidt, the Manager.

MANAGER   Well, we do all we can at Universal Products to keep our workers happy.

TERRY   Happy, happy, always happy.

MANAGER   Radio One all day, two canteens ... manual and clerical ...

TERRY   Dirty and clean.

MANAGER   Sports and social club.

TERRY   And still a few bob left for wages, it's amazing ... but what about the work?

MANAGER   That's for us to say. We look after you but there comes a point where you've just got to do as we ask.

TERRY   Why?

MANAGER   The system. You can't fight the system.

TERRY   What about the people that own the system?

MANAGER   That's economics, lad, not for the likes of you and me to discuss economics.

TERRY   I bet the people that run the system spend all their days whittling, and whittling, and whittling ...

He walks into the coffee bar area, where Dave is sitting. This starts a realistic scene and ends the series of impressions.

DAVE What's up kid?

TERRY (*shrugging*) The lot!

DAVE How are you doing?

TERRY Terrible.

DAVE Still out of work?

TERRY Nobody wants people like me.

DAVE Prospects?

TERRY My Dad fixed up for me to see his foreman, he's made this appointment for me . . .

DAVE When for?

There is a pause

TERRY Twenty minutes ago.

DAVE You forgot it?

TERRY Looks like it.

DAVE Well, forget it.

TERRY I have done. (*Pause*) You get something better?

DAVE I got something better.

TERRY My Dad'll go berserk.

DAVE What's the odds? Anybody that isn't berserk these days must be insane.

TERRY My Mam'll be dead choked as well.

DAVE (*sharply*) Forget it!

TERRY (*to the camera*) So I forgot it.

Exterior of a fairground by night

A sequence of fairground shots, briefly establishing the scene and atmosphere.

A hot-dog stall

The fairground noises can be heard. Terry is alone in a small mobile hot-dog stall.

TERRY (*selling*) Here we are then. Get your hot dogs, get your lovely hot dogs, get your lovely hot dogs, with or without onions, with choice of two kinds of sauce, one full, one empty . . .

He turns to look at the camera, suddenly aware of being watched.
. . . . I'll tell you about this job: Dave fixed it, you see, it's a mate of his runs it . . . he's got about six of these stalls, sort of a tycoon he is . . . I'll tell you what I have to do. (*He demonstrates*) These are your bread rolls, see? Slice your bread roll . . . I generally get a few dozen ready, for when it gets busy later on, especially after the pubs close . . . slice your bread roll, pop the banger in . . . onion down that side . . . tomato sauce down the other side . . . pop it in a paper bag . . . and there you are . . . One shilling, sir, if you please . . . (*He sells it to a passing customer*) I charge one and six when it's busy . . . keep the difference. The boss says it's OK but pay my own insurance. (*Changing his voice.*) Now I know what you're all saying . . .
Cut to a close shot of his Dad.

DAD   You could have had a perfectly good job in the station.

TERRY I can make twice as much on this job.
Cut to a close shot of his Mum.

MUM   I thought you got bored doing the same thing over and over again.

TERRY Yes, but this is just for a week. And then it stops. What makes it all right is knowing it's going to stop. With other jobs, it only stops when you retire.
Cut to a close shot of Maitland.

MAITLAND But what about your future?

TERRY I'm fed up of people telling me to think about tomorrow. They tell you to put up with being miserable today, it'll all be lovely in five years time . . . I want it now, mate . . .
Cut to a close shot of the Manager.

MANAGER But you can't beat the system.

TERRY Maybe it's time somebody had a go. Sunshine for everybody.
Cut to a close shot of Janie.

JANIE What about me Terry?

TERRY You *are* my sunshine. And you'll have to put up with me. Well she will won't she? She's got the best chance of winning in the end. Maybe they'll all win in the end . . .

I don't know . . . that's tomorrow and I don't know about tomorrow. But I'll tell you this for nothing, mateys . . . right now, this very minute . . . it's hot dogs, hot dogs, get your lovely hot dogs . . . because I say it is . . . and there's nobody on this earth can take that away from me. (*And he carries on preparing his hot dogs behind the credits— a happy man.*)

Hero in the Dust

by Rex Edwards

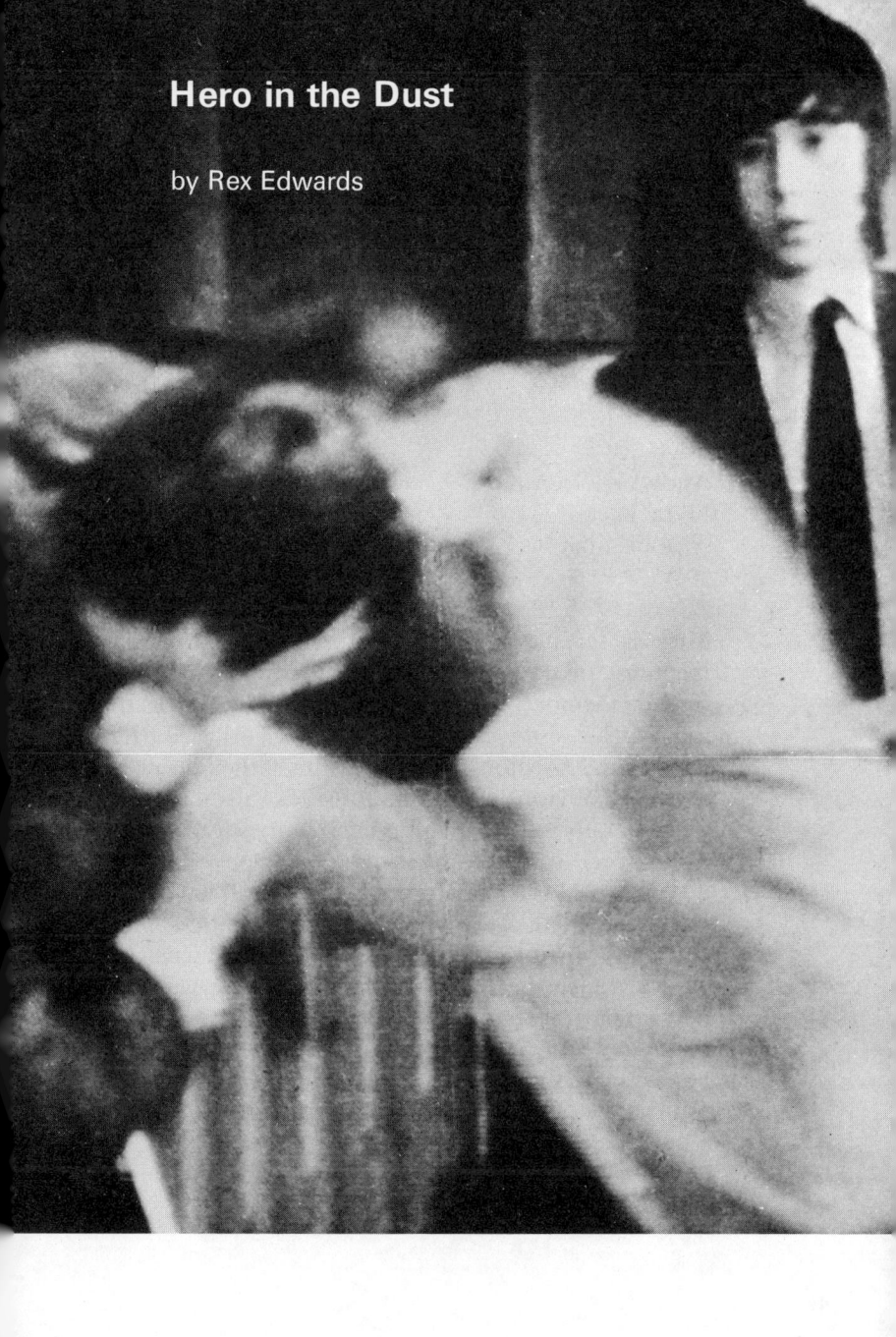

The Cast

Barney Judd, *warden of the youth club*
Mick, *a past member*
Sally, *his sister*
Mrs Bonner
Mr Bonner *their parents*
Spike } *Mick's friends*
Ginger
Dave
Andy } *club members*
Myra
A policeman

Mick is seventeen and a troublemaker, particularly at meetings of the Chequers Youth Club of which he was once a member. The matter is complicated by the fact that Mick's sister, Sally, is the girl friend of Barney, the club leader. At home, Mick and his father don't get on, and Mick obviously feels that his sister Sally is the favourite of the family—for one thing she is more successful than he is.

Mick and his two mates try to gate-crash the club dance, fight and break a window. The club members, including Sally, are all for calling the police, but Barney refuses. He obviously believes Mick is struggling with a better nature. He also thinks Mick has a sense of inferiority about his sister. By the end of the play both Mick and Barney are shaken. Mick is again in the hands of the police. We feel that it may be the beginning, though, of a new life for him.

Hero in the Dust

Outside a Youth Club

It is evening. Three boys appear in the shot. They are dressed roughly. Mick is an apparently tough, aggressive seventeen year-old, but with a hint of a sensitive personality beneath the arrogant exterior. He is the leader. Ginger is younger, good looking; Spike is tough, powerfully built, slower than the others.

They stand ready for action. Mick nods, with a taut grin. The boys move away. We cut to a view of a wall. They come into the shot. Spike takes a firework from his pocket; Mick tosses the firework through an open window, then walks cockily into the club with his companions.

Inside the Youth Club

The Youth Club has a common-room, entrance passage, club office and part of kitchen. We open on the common-room, a large room with doors leading to entrance passage and to kitchen. A table-tennis table is at one end, with two teenage boys playing and others watching, including Andy. Nearer the camera is a record-player, with some teenage girls dancing to the music; one of these, an attractive, cheerful character, is Myra.

A dart-board is against one wall, and there is a coffee bar at one end. The furniture is mainly light folding-chairs and tables. Two or three posters announce an inter-club table-tennis tournament, the next club ramble, a forthcoming dance, etc.

There is a sudden loud explosion.

A girl gives a little scream. Everyone alerts. Mick, Spike and Ginger appear at the door. They grin, pleased at the general alarm, then swagger into the room.

In the club office Barney Judd, the club-leader, had been working at his desk. Barney is in his late twenties, intelligent, athletic. He looks up, frowning. The door opens and a club member, Dave (not previously seen) comes in.

DAVE Hey, Barney! It's Mick.

BARNEY   Who?

DAVE   Mick Bonner. He threw a firework in the toilet.

Barney gets up, leaves the room, followed by Dave.

In the common-room Mick and Ginger have taken over the table-tennis table and are beginning their game. Spike watches, smoking a cigarette.

Barney enters, with Dave. He switches off the record-player and the music stops. Barney goes up to Mick, the club members watching.

BARNEY   Mick. Just a minute.

MICK   (*engrossed in his game*) I'm busy.

ANDY   It was our game. They barged in.

BARNEY   Someone threw a firework. Was it you?

MICK   (*innocent*) Me? . . . Oh, Mr Judd.

DAVE   It must have been you. I was in the toilet. You threw a firework in the window.

MICK   What's up? . . . You get blown down the hole?

Spike and Ginger laugh.

BARNEY   Outside. All three of you.

MICK   Eh? We're members.

SPIKE   Yeh.

GINGER   Yeh, course.

BARNEY   You've been barred, and you know it. That firework could have caused an injury. I'm barring you for another month.

MICK   We've been playing table-tennis.

BARNEY   Put those bats down.

MICK   (*still playing*) After the game.

BARNEY   You heard me! (*Annoyed, he takes the table-tennis bat from Mick*) O.K. Outside.

MICK   (*frowning*) Do you want bother?

BARNEY   (*levelly*) Not unless you do.

There is a pause. They glare at each other, then Mick gives in.

MICK   Who wants this sissy joint, anyway? (*To the others*) Come on, let's go somewhere decent.

Ginger offers the table-tennis bat to Andy. Andy goes to take it, but Ginger pokes him in the midriff with it then tosses the bat down the room. Spike deliberately treads on the table-tennis ball. With a shove of his foot, Mick pushes the table out of place then marches out, escorted by Barney and followed by his friends. Mick exchanges a look with Myra as he leaves the room; Mick is frowning, defiant; Myra concerned, rather unhappy. In the passage, Barney pauses by his office door.

BARNEY Come back when you've grown up a bit.

MICK (*marching on*) Get lost.

Barney goes back into clubroom. Music starts up again.

As the three boys are about to leave, Sally Bonner, Mick's sister, enters from the street. Sally is a good-looking girl in her early twenties, an intelligent, rather studious type, and a distinct cut above Mick.

Mick gives Sally a contemptuous look.

MICK It's Dolly Do-good.

He barges noisily out through the main door, followed by the others. Sally goes into office. Barney enters.

BARNEY Hi, Sally.

SALLY Hi. More trouble?

BARNEY Throwing fireworks.

SALLY They're a pain in the neck.

During dialogue, Sally removes her hat and coat and hangs them on the coat-hanger; Barney sorts through his papers.

BARNEY Mick was always a hard case. But till you came here at least he tried to behave.

SALLY So I should stay away because my brother's a moron?

BARNEY He's a good kid. I don't get it.

SALLY He's a hooligan. He plagues this club, he causes upsets at home and he's getting a name in the district.

BARNEY Sure. But why?

SALLY I told you why. He's a thug.

BARNEY (*doubtful*) Mm . . .

SALLY You're too soft with him, Barney. If he shows up again, send for the police.

BARNEY (*shakes his head*) Uh-uh.

SALLY You'll have to, one day.

BARNEY (*a shrug*) Maybe.

SALLY You will. (*Preparing to go*) Cup of coffee?

BARNEY Just the job.

Sally gives him a smile, goes out.

The Bonners' living room

We open on tea being poured into a cup, then pull back to show the living-room. Mick's mother, Mrs Bonner—a homely, good-natured woman in her forties—is pouring the tea. Also seated at the table taking their evening meal, are Mick and Mick's father, Sid Bonner —fiftyish, a factory-worker, a good-living man, rather strait-laced.

BONNER *(referring to Mick)* So he's out of a job, now.

MRS B. *(resigned, not unhappy)* Oh, well.

BONNER *(to Mick)* Why?

MICK *(not looking at his father)* Got the sack.

BONNER *(annoyed)* But what happened?

MICK Had a row with the gaffer, didn't I.

BONNER You're always having rows! . . . Can't hold a job five minutes.

We hear the front door closing.

MRS B. Never mind, Sid.

BONNER I do mind! He's on the labour, again.

MICK Jobs are two a penny.

BONNER Your sort are. Why don't you get a good job, for once?

MICK Pay my way, don't I?

BONNER I could get you on at our place—you could learn instrument-making—

MICK Me and five thousand others.

BONNER I wouldn't recommend you, though. Fine thing, isn't it? A man can't recommend his own son.

MICK *(grieved)* Don't. I can't bear it.

MRS B. Stop that, Mick. Eat your dinner.
Sally enters.

SALLY *(bright)* Hullo.

MRS B. Hullo, dear. Sit down—I'll get you dinner.
Sally sits at the table; Mrs Bonner goes out to the kitchen. Mick ignores his sister; he gets up, moves to the window, lights a cigarette. Mr Bonner takes a small cardboard box from the jacket hanging on the back of his chair and pushes it across to Sally. Bonner has little time for Mick. but his manner towards Sally is warm, friendly.

BONNER   Here, Sally. For your young man.
         Sally opens the box, takes out an old-fashioned silver watch.
SALLY   Oh, you've repaired it! Thanks Dad. How much?
BONNER   Nothing—I did it in my lunch break. Grand watch, that. Don't see that quality, nowadays.
SALLY   It was Barney's grandfather's handed down. Thanks a lot—that's great.
         Mrs Bonner enters during this, with Sally's meal. Mick is fiddling with the radio; he gives the watch a glance, but doesn't speak.
MRS B.   You going to the club tonight, Sally?
SALLY   (*nods*) We've got a dance. Thank you, Mum. (*A pointed glance at Mick.*) Hope we don't have any more trouble with fireworks.
BONNER   Eh? (*Blaring pop music is suddenly heard.*)
BONNER   Turn that off! . . . Mick!
MICK   What?
BONNER   Turn it off. It's tripe.
         Mick gives a cool look at his father. He turns up the volume, then walks out of the room, slamming the door.
BONNER   (*angry*) Hey, come back! . . . I'll teach you!
MRS B.   (*mollifying*) Sid. (*She turns off the radio.*)
BONNER   (*muttering*) Bloomin' freak. What would you do with him? (*To Sally, a softer tone.*) You said something about fireworks . . .
SALLY   Er. No, it's O.K.
BONNER   Was it young Mick? . . . More hooliganism?
SALLY   Dad. It doesn't matter.
         Bonner frowns. Sally exchanges a glance with her mother, and applies herself to her meal.

The Youth Club that night

The members are dancing in the common-room. A small table stands near the entrance to the common-room, a cash-box and a roll of tickets on it. Barney leaves table and goes into hall. Dave stands by the table, talking to Myra.
The main door is thrown open and Mick, Ginger and Spike walk in.

DAVE   (*apprehensive*) Oh-oh . . .
       Mick and the others swagger up to the table.
MICK   Three tickets.
DAVE   It's members only.
       Mick grabs Dave by his lapels, pushes him back against the wall.
MYRA   Mick, don't be a nit!
MICK   (*to Dave*) Three tickets—right?
DAVE   (*struggling free*) Lay off! It's members only.
MICK   (*angry*) Come on! (*He throws money on the table.*)
DAVE   You're not going in.
SPIKE   Belt him, Mick.
GINGER   Yeh, go on.
MYRA   (*pleading*) Don't make trouble Mick, please.
MICK   We wanna dance, that's all.
MYRA   You started a fight last time, didn't you.
DAVE   I'll get Barney.
MYRA   No, wait. (*To Mick cajoling*) Look, let's go down the caff, eh? I'll skip the dance.
MICK   See you inside, Myra.
       Mick and the other two move to go into the common-room. As they do so, Barney appears at the door, barring their way.
BARNEY   What's going on?
DAVE   They tried to barge in.
BARNEY   Sorry, boys.
MICK   Now, look—we paid money—
BARNEY   Here's your money. (*Takes the coins from the table, gives them to Mick.*) Come on, now please.
       Barney takes Mick's arm. Sally appears from the common-room, some of the club members behind her. The dance-music has stopped.
MICK   (*wrenching free*) Leave go of me!
SALLY   Barney, shall I—
BARNEY   It's O.K. All right, lads.
       He starts to urge them towards the door. Mick pushes the table over; the money spills on the floor. Ginger tears a poster from the wall.
SALLY   I'll get the police.
MICK   You do that!
BARNEY   No!

MICK I dare you!

DAVE (*to the members*) Hey, fellers!

Dave and two or three of the members grapple with Spike and Ginger and throw them out.

Mick goes to his friends' aid but Barney stops him.

BARNEY (*to Dave*) Now hold it, hold it.

He whips open the office door and thrusts Mick in.

MICK What's the idea?

BARNEY Lay off this club.

MICK Let me out!

BARNEY Stay away from here. We're losing members, because of you, and I'm fed up with it.

MICK Get away from that door!

BARNEY You're not as "thick" as you make out. Be yourself. Stop trying to be a hard nut. You're no Al Capone.

Mick holds up his clenched fist.

MICK You want this?

BARNEY Don't be stupid.

MICK I'd do it, you know. Dare me—go on, dare me.

BARNEY Grow up, Mick, will you?

MICK You're keeping me here while my sister gets the cops.

BARNEY I'm asking you to behave like a responsible club member.

MICK You get stuffed!

There is a crash of glass. A window has been broken.

BARNEY That's Spike or Ginger. Do us a favour, will you? Get out and stay out.

He opens the door. Mick pauses, then glowers at Barney and goes out.

Sally, Dave, Myra and one or two others are in the passage; Mick gives them a frowning glance, pushes through them, leaves the club.

SALLY They broke a window.

BARNEY (*nods*).

DAVE We should've called the police.

There are murmurs of agreement from the other members, except Myra.

BARNEY That's not the way. They'd act up even more.

DAVE We should have. They think we're soft. (*A rather scornful look at Barney.*) Perhaps we are.

A pause, then Dave, Myra, and the others return to the common-room.

SALLY So you'll let Mick get away with it? You'll let him smash up the club?

BARNEY It's not only Mick.

SALLY He's the ringleader.

BARNEY Look, we won't solve this by calling the police.

SALLY Then *how* will we?

BARNEY I don't know. Any suggestions?

SALLY You're the club leader.

BARNEY I may be the club leader but it's their club.

A pause, then the dance music starts up again. Sally gives Barney a serious and rather unhappy look; then goes into the common-room. Barney shrugs, sits at the table.

The Bonners' living room that evening

Mrs Bonner sits at the now cleared table, worried, preoccupied, absently picking at the cloth. Mr Bonner is winding the alarm-clock.

BONNER (*frowning*) Half-past eleven.

MRS B. You go to bed, Sid. I'll wait.

BONNER We'll both wait.

He replaces the clock on the mantelshelf, lights a cigarette, thinking the while.

BONNER I just don't get him. . .

MRS B. He'll grow out of it. They all do.

BONNER He'll grow into a bloomin' crook! . . . This is the start—don't you see?

MRS B. But it wasn't a *crime*, Sid.

BONNER The police think so! My stars, blokes like him are sup-posed to come from *bad* homes.

MRS B. A lot of youngsters are wild, these days.

BONNER They're not all like Mick, though! . . . And when you think of Sally . . . grammar school—good job—helping out at that club. Mick, he was even a flop at the secondary school . . . and all he can do is cause trouble.

MRS B.   Sally was always your favourite.

BONNER   Can you blame me? . . . Can you blame me? (*Pause*) I
          don't get him. I just don't understand . . .

          The front door can be heard closing.

          *Mrs Bonner looks up, waiting. She gives a worried glance at her
          husband. The door opens, and Mick enters. He pauses, surprised
          to see them.*

MICK   Thought you'd be in bed.

BONNER   (*hostile*) Where've you been?

MICK   Eh?

BONNER   This evening. Where've you been, what you been up to?

MICK   Out with my mates, that's all.

MRS B.   (*concerned*) Yes, but where, Mick?

MICK   Oh . . . Down to the Chequers. Tried to get in the dance
          but they wouldn't let us in.

BONNER   Then what?

MICK   (*a frown*) Why all the questions?

BONNER   Answer me!

MRS B.   Mick. Where did you go, after you left the club?

MICK   The caff.

MRS B.   And then where?

MICK   (*stonewalling*) Got any supper? Got any cheese?

BONNER   Answer, will you!

MICK   Why should I?

BONNER   Because the police have been here . . .

MICK   (*after a pause*) About the club?

BONNER   You took a car. (*Pause*) You stole a car, you and your
          mates. You were recognized.

          *A pause. Mick looks at his mother. Bonner lifts his jacket from the
          back of his chair, puts it on.*

BONNER   Come on. We've got to go down to the station.

The Youth Club

*Barney stands at the coffee bar drinking a cup of coffee poured out
for him by Myra. Myra is now setting out cups and saucers ready
for the evening's session. It is early, and there are no members in
the club as yet.*

BARNEY Probation?

MYRA And a fine. The beak said next time it's Borstal.

BARNEY But they didn't really steal the car?

MYRA Oh, no! It was a joyride. Mick said it was the chap's own fault—he left his keys in.

BARNEY Some excuse!

MYRA I think they "dared" him—you know, Ginger and Spike. Mick's like that—if he's dared to do something he just has to do it.

BARNEY Bit childish, isn't it? (*Myra shrugs.*) You were his girl once, weren't you, Myra?

MYRA Mm. Till he got grotty—you know, acting up. I still like him. He's a good bloke, really but . . . he just don't care.

BARNEY Doesn't care about what?

MYRA Oh . . . anything. He says everything's crummy, everyone's on the make. He likes—you know—larking about with the gang, messing things up.
Dave appears.

DAVE Hi, Myra. Is the coffee on?

MYRA (*pouring the coffee*) Sure.

BARNEY Evening, Dave.

DAVE (*rather cool*) Evening, Mr Judd.

BARNEY You O.K. for Friday? Members' committee meeting.

DAVE Er . . . Well yeh, I'll come Friday; But I might be resigning, later on.

BARNEY Why's this?

DAVE Oh . . . er . . . Just things, Mr Judd . . . Thanks Myra.
Dave hands over some money, takes his coffee, and moves away. More club members have arrived in the common-room and the sound of a table-tennis game is heard.

BARNEY (*to Myra*) Mr Judd? Not Barney.

MYRA Er . . . No.
She gives Barney a look, looks away. Barney smiles to himself, finishes his coffee.

The Bonners' kitchen

Mrs Bonner is at the sink, wiping a cup and saucer. A door closes.

MRS B. That you, Sally?

MICK (*heard off*) It's me.

He enters from the living-room. He is rather glum, bored with himself.

MRS B. You're early?

MICK Got fed up, nothing to do. Where's the old man?

MRS B. Don't call him that. Your Dad's gone to bed.

MICK (*not really interested*) Mm. (*Indicating a plate of sandwiches*) Who're these for? Sally?

MRS B. Both of you.

MICK That makes a change.

MRS B. What d'you mean?

MICK Well, it's usually all "Sally" in this house, isn't it?

MRS B. Not with me, it isn't.

MICK It is with the old—it is with Dad. What's he gone to bed for? Get out of my way?

MRS B. He was tired. He's on overtime.

MICK Got any cocoa?

MRS B. Yes, sure.

Mrs Bonner puts the milk on, makes the cocoa, during the dialogue. Mick sits at the table, glances at a newspaper, eats a sandwich.

MRS B. You go to the Probation Office, this evening?

MICK Yeh.

MRS B. What did they say?

MICK Oh, just chat. Want me to get a job.

MRS B. Well, of course, Mick!

MICK Ah, who cares about jobs. All jobs are for is to keep you tied down where you were born.

MRS B. You've got to live, haven't you? You'll get married, one day, raise a family.

MICK Yeh. Live thirty years in a council house then, finish up in an old folks' home.

MRS B. That's silly talk.

MICK Dead right. They'll start a war, before that.

MRS B. (*after a pause*) You've got 'em tonight, haven't you . . .

MICK (*almost inaudible*) So what?

Mrs Bonner looks at Mick, as he sits disinterestedly leafing through the newspaper.

MRS B. (*sympathetic*) What's the matter, son?

MICK (*looking up*) Mm? . . . (*Looks down at the paper, again*) Nothing. Everything . . .

MRS B. Something happen, this evening?

MICK Only the copper.

MRS B. Oh? What's this?

MICK Well . . . We're on this bridge, see. You know, the canal, near the club. We're doing nothing—*nothing*. Then up comes this cop and moves us on.

MRS B. There must be a reason.

MICK Well, they got the mockers on us, ain't they? For ever and ever, goodnight, amen.

MRS B. I expect he thought you were up to something with the club again.

MICK Yeh, he did. But we weren't.

MRS B. Can't blame him, though, can you?

MICK We'll fix that club. It was someone there put him up to it.

MRS B. You don't *know* that!

MICK It must've been. Spike said . . . We'll fix that dump, for good.

MRS B. Stop that, now! . . . You think you're big, don't you, you and your gang. What good are you, to anyone? Where's it going to end?

Mick glowers at his mother, then returns to his newspaper.

MICK Let's have that cocoa, Ma.

Mrs Bonner gives a sad shake of her head.

The Youth Club

In Barney's office: the members' committee meeting is in progress, attended by Barney, Sally, Dave, Andy, Myra and two or three other club members. Pop music can be faintly heard from the common-room. Barney has a file of papers on his knee. He looks at his watch.

BARNEY Getting late. Any other business?

SALLY (*consulting her notebook*) Last item. The anniversary dance, this Saturday. Dave wants to raise something.

DAVE Yeh. (*to Barney*) We wondered if you could tell the police.

BARNEY Tell 'em what?

DAVE   Ask 'em to look in now and again, during the dance. (*A quick glance at Sally then away*) We might have visitors, see.

BARNEY   You mean Mick?

DAVE   And Spike and Ginger. Myra heard they might come down and have a giggle.

SALLY   For heaven's sake! . . . It's the club's birthday party—the last night we want trouble.

ANDY   We don't want the police around either.

MYRA   But we have to do something. I mean, they could really mess it up.

SALLY   I'll speak to Mick, read the Riot Act.

DAVE   It wants more than that, Sally. It wants the police.

BARNEY   Now, I'm sure you don't mean . . .

DAVE   (*frowning*) I don't mean what? Are you gonna let 'em come in, and have a ball?

BARNEY   Could be.
There is a howl of protest from the others.

SALLY   You don't seriously think . . .

BARNEY   Now look. We've tried the big stick. I've suspended them—twice. That doesn't seem to work; they still want to come here—for a giggle. Perhaps we ought to try another way.

SALLY   Such as.

BARNEY   Sweet reason. I could go and see Mick, and the other two, at home and, well . . . offer the olive branch.

SALLY   They'd hit you with it.

BARNEY   They might respond. Look—part of the reason they needle us is because we keep 'em out.

DAVE   Well, yeh, we don't want 'em.

BARNEY   So they force themselves on us. Honestly there is a good side to them. There is to everybody. Let me have a try to appeal to it.
The committee members look at one another. Barney's suggestion has taken them by surprise. Except for Andy.

ANDY   I've got a better idea; We'll be having our get together before the dance—this committee, you know coffee and cakes and all that. We'll ask them to that.
Barney looks surprised.

ANDY You say it's our club. Why should you do all the dirty work? We'll all offer the olive branch.

DAVE Have you gone round the twist, mate?

BARNEY Well, you'll need to be very careful what you say . . .

ANDY We'll be careful.

BARNEY I suppose we might make progress.

SALLY They won't come.

ANDY Then we win either way. If they do come we've got a chance of getting things back to normal. If they refuse well then we've made the offer and they're not so likely to barge in and try to smash the dance up.

SALLY I can't see Mick accepting an invitation to coffee and cakes.

ANDY Then dare him to come.

BARNEY (*a smile*) You're always telling me he can't refuse a dare! Well then Andy's proposed a motion that we invite the lads to meet us all before the dance on Saturday.

MYRA I'll second it.

BARNEY Those in favour.

A pause during which Andy and Myra raise their hands. Then the others do except for Sally and Dave.

SALLY I'll stay neutral.

DAVE And I think it's daft.

BARNEY Majority in favour. Motion carried. We invite them.

A patch of waste-ground

Mick, Spike and Ginger are lounging, discussing the situation.

SPIKE I think it's a con.

GINGER Course it is.

MICK If they start, we start.

SPIKE They'll get the cops down, and hang something on us.

GINGER Yeh. I vote we skip it.

MICK What's the matter? Scared?

GINGER Look, mate, a nosh up. Why? 'Cause they love us?

MICK My sister said they wanna chat.

SPIKE (*scornful*) Chat!

MICK   We're going. We'll drink their rotten coffee, have a giggle, then push off. What's to lose?

SPIKE   Er . . . O.K. But if they start anything we give it back—right? We take 'em apart.

MICK   Well, that's fair enough. Nobody slaps us down. But nobody! (*He eases himself up*) Come on, let's get going.
The three boys move away from camera.

The Youth Club—day

The common-room. A trestle-table has been covered with a cloth, and places laid for the club people and their guests. Barney is putting chairs in place. Sally gives the final touches to the table (e.g. arranging flowers). The room has been decorated and hung with balloons etc. in preparation for the evening's dance; Dave and Andy are fixing the final decorations into place, another committee member sorts through gramophone records. Myra and another girl come from the kitchen with refreshments.

BARNEY   Mick's trouble is, he has to be the boss.

SALLY   Of a tinpot little gang?

BARNEY   Of anything, any situation. He wants to get somewhere, amount to something. He's got the spirit, but he doesn't know how.

SALLY   I'd just like to see some good in him.

BARNEY   There is good. If it came to the crunch, he'd prove it.

SALLY   You believe in him—I live with him. There are two things you can do with tearaways—write them off, or cut them down to size.

BARNEY   With Mick, there's a third way. You could break his authority over the other two lads, split up the gang, tip their hero in the dust. He might come to his senses, then—and I could give him some authority here where it's more use.

SALLY   How do we go about it?

BARNEY   (*a shrug*) Search me.
Dave has finished the decorations, and comes over. He has overheard the last remarks.

DAVE   Everything's ready. They're late. Let's hope they don't come, eh?

At that moment the sound of the main door is heard being violently thrown back.

BARNEY (*drily*) The guests have arrived.

Mick, Spike and Ginger come swaggering into the room, stare insolently around.

BARNEY Hi, boys. Nice to see you.

MICK (*dead-pan*) Yeh.

BARNEY Tea's all ready. Have a seat.

MICK What's the fiddle?

BARNEY Mm?

MICK You hate our guts. (*Gestures at the tea-table.*) Why all this?

BARNEY We don't like the way you act up, sometimes—but we certainly don't hate you. We'd like to talk things over. Any objections?

Mick frowns, looks at Spike and Ginger. Spike shrugs; Mick pulls a chair out.

MICK We'll stay for the nosh.

A pause, then all seat themselves. Myra brings over the coffee and hands it round. There is rather tense, edgy atmosphere, the club members and the gang watching each other suspiciously.

BARNEY (*over this*) Incidentally if you'd like to stay on for the dance this evening we'd like to have you.

DAVE (*a mutter*) We'd get you, anyway.

MICK What?

DAVE If we don't invite you, you'll gate-crash, start a rumpus. We're stuck with you.

MICK So *that*'s the fiddle.

BARNEY (*annoyed with Dave*) Not really. We'd like to make a fresh start. It does no one any good, fighting. We suggest we call it a day.

ANDY Yeh, that's right.

Mick looks at Barney but says nothing. He pours coffee into his saucer and begins noisily to sip it.

SALLY (*in protest*) Mick!

MICK (*coolly*) Something the matter?

SALLY Drink it properly. You'd never do that at home

Mick continues sipping.

BARNEY How about it, Mick? We're prepared to bury the hatchet, and invite you to come back to the club.

MICK (*sarcastically*) Really.

SALLY On one condition.

MICK Oh?

SALLY That you behave like human beings.

Mick "accidentally" drops his saucer; it smashes. Spike and Ginger grin.

MICK (*pretending to be surprised and contrite*) Oh, sorry. Dropped it.

There is a pause.

BARNEY Well? What do you say?

MICK Mm?

BARNEY About the club.

MICK You can have your sissy club.

GINGER Yeh.

SPIKE You can stuff it.

BARNEY Why's this?

MICK I told you; It's sissy.

BARNEY What's sissy about it?

MICK Everything. (*He gestures at the decorations, the tea-table.*) All this.

BARNEY Well, if you were a member again, you could do something about it, couldn't you?

MICK Dead right, man.

SALLY And what would you do?

MICK I'd smash this sissy china, for a start.

BARNEY Go on?

MICK Every flippin' bit.

BARNEY Mm-hm. (*He pushes an empty cup and saucer towards Mick.*) Show me.

MICK (*a frown of surprise*) Eh?

BARNEY You said you'd smash the sissy china. Go ahead.

SALLY (*concerned*) Barney—

DAVE Yeh—

BARNEY Smash that cup and saucer. I dare you.

Mick hasn't expected this development, but he gives a cocky grin at Spike and Ginger, then takes the cup and smashes it to the floor.

BARNEY A good start. But that's only the cup.

63

There is a momentary pause, then Mick smashes the saucer, also. There are murmurs of protest from the club people.

SALLY Barney, what's the idea?

BARNEY Just a moment. (*He pushes another cup and saucer before Mick.*) Every bit, you said. Carry on. (*Mick is now rather uneasy.*) I dare you.

Mick impulsively picks up cup and saucer and hurls them to the floor.

DAVE (*to Barney*) That's club property!

The others add their protests.

BARNEY (*calmly*) It's O.K. Everything that's smashed I'll replace out of my own pocket.

MICK Don't bother. (*He rises, preparing to go.*) O.K., fellers.

Spike and Ginger rise too.

BARNEY Oh. Playing chicken, eh?

MICK NO!

BARNEY Then smash. Smash everything. Make a clean sweep of the table.

DAVE (*agitated*) Barney.

BARNEY (*to Mick*) I dare you. We won't raise a finger—I promise.

Mick is tensed, under emotion. Barney gets up from the table; Sally and the others do likewise, not knowing what to expect.

SPIKE (*uneasy*) Let's go, Mick.

BARNEY I dare you to do it.

Mick gulps, then seizes the table-cloth and sweeps everything on it to the floor.

MICK (*a defiant shout*) O.K.?

Who's chicken?

BARNEY (*appreciative*) Great!

Apprehensive, not understanding the strange situation, Spike and Ginger edge towards the door. The others stare at Barney and Mick, wondering at the next development.

Barney takes his old-fashioned silver watch from his pocket and lays it on the bare table.

BARNEY My old watch. Used to be my grandad's. Went all through the navy with me. I'm very fond of this watch. (*He takes up a hammer used for fixing the decorations, lays it beside the watch*). Smash it.

Mick stares at Barney, bewildered, breathing quickly.

BARNEY   Go on. I give you my word there'll be no come-back—
even if you smash it to smithereens.
Mick's mental torment shows on his face, but he makes no move.

BARNEY   I dare you. I dare you to smash that watch.
*A little sound comes from Mick, expressing his tension. He picks
up a chair, throws it violently to the floor.*

BARNEY   (*calm*) It's not the watch.
*Mick stares around him, tears the dart-board from its moorings,
throws it down.*

BARNEY   It's not the watch!
*Dave and some of the members have left the room. Confused,
beside himself, Mick hurls furniture about, pulls more decorations
down, but he cannot bring himself to smash the watch. Barney
pursues him relentlessly.*

BARNEY   The watch!... I dare you! Smash the watch!

MICK   (*turning, at bay*) Shut up! Shut up! (*Calls to Spike and Ginger*)
Do 'em, can't you? Do 'em!
Mick snatches up the hammer, raises it.

SALLY   Mick!
*Myra gives a scream. Spike and Ginger, very scared, slip out of the
room. Barney faces Mick.*

BARNEY   Go on!... I dare you!
*Mick gives an inarticulate cry, then throws the hammer from him.
He hurls himself at Barney, punching wildly. Barney grapples
with Mick, trying to restrain him.*

SALLY   Barney!... Barney—Mick—
*A policeman has entered the common-room, Dave and the others
behind him. The policeman comes forward.*

POLICE-
MAN   All right, Bonner!

MICK   (*swinging round*) I knew it!... A trick! You laid it on!

BARNEY   (*frowning*) No!

MICK   Then *she* did! (*indicates Sally.*)

POLICE-
MAN   I'll have to take him, Mr Judd. We know him of old. (*Takes
Mick's arm*) Come on, you.

MICK   (*struggling*) Get off!

MYRA   Mick! . . . Please!

Mick struggles a moment, trying to free himself, then suddenly gives in.

MICK   Ah, what's the use . ...

He is hopeless, despairing, all his fire and anger gone. Barney turns to the policeman.

BARNEY   It's O.K. It wasn't his fault.

POLICE-
MAN   I saw him, didn't I?

BARNEY   Yes—but he was provoked—I provoked him; I provoked him.

POLICE-
MAN   Sorry. He'll have to come to the station.

BARNEY   But look, I'm not laying any charges.

POLICE-
MAN   What's the matter with you? We know this chap. There's been charges laid against him and we're obliged to look into them.

BARNEY   I'll speak for him. I'll go bail for him.

POLICE-
MAN   You can do what you like—but he'll have to come with me. (*To Mick*) All right, son.

The policeman takes Mick's arm; they go towards the door. Mick pauses when he comes to Sally; he stares at her, fierce, angry, accusing. Then he turns from his sister and goes out with the policeman. Confused, distressed, Sally turns to Barney.

SALLY   Well?

Barney doesn't answer, the incident has shaken him. He picks up the watch, glances at it, puts it in his pocket. He takes a look at the wrecked room, then turns to go to the door. He pauses, looks at Sally.

BARNEY   You coming to the station with me?

SALLY   Yes.

They go out. Dave, Myra and the members look at one another, at a loss what to do or say, then Myra turns and goes out after Sally and Barney. Andy looks at Dave, querying; Dave shrugs.

DAVE   (*to departing Barney*) Which hero, Mr Judd?

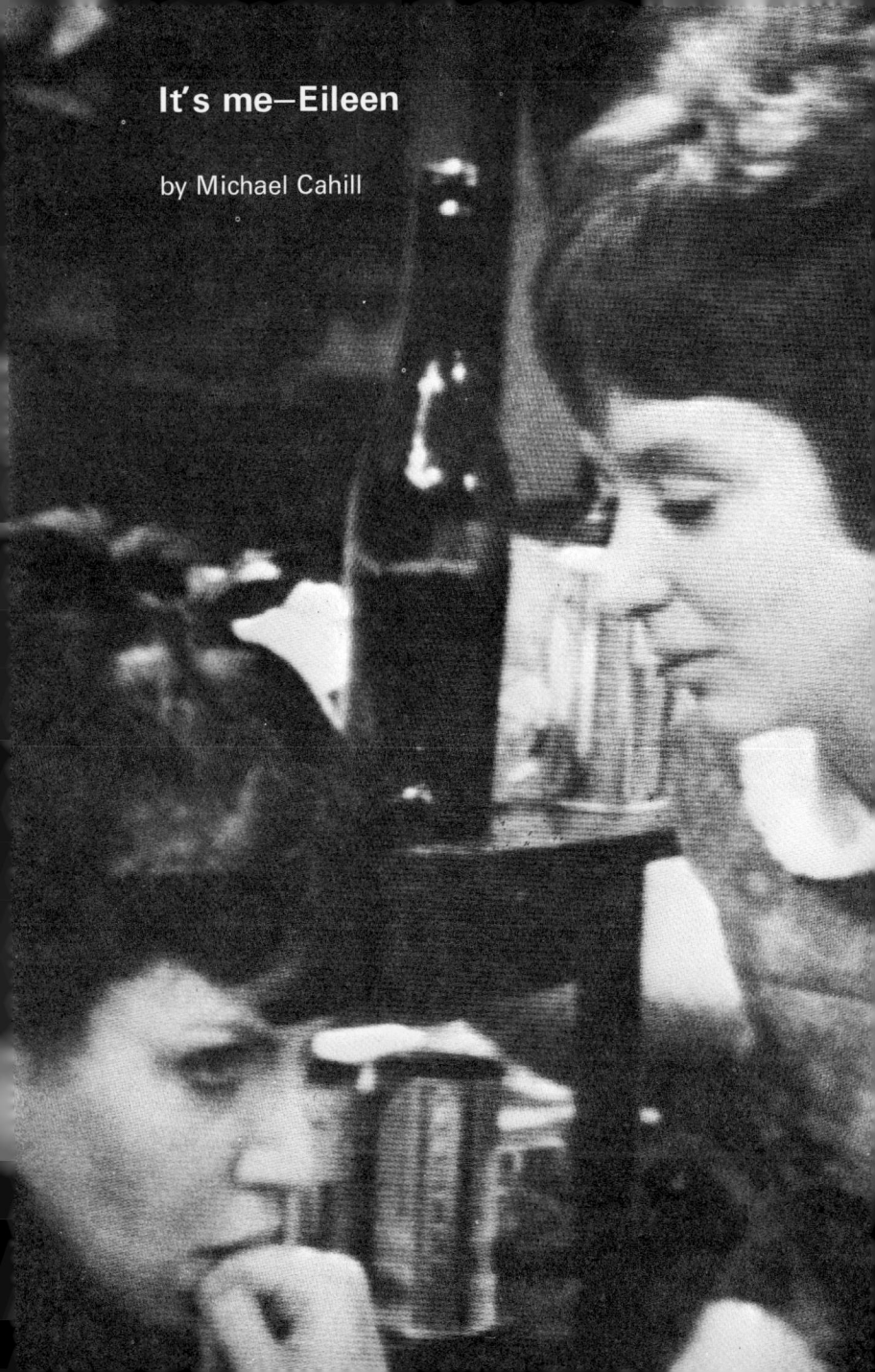

It's me—Eileen

by Michael Cahill

The Cast

Eileen
Her mother
Her father
Jimmy, her brother
Deana
Angela } *Deana's friends*
Peter }

Life for Eileen at home seems so uninteresting that she often doesn't get up until after lunch at weekends, and she feels so restricted by her mother's worries about her that she is often unhappy. Eileen is seventeen and out at work: family life seems to be worse than useless.

Her friend from work, Deana, seems to have a far better life. She lives in a small flat, can run her own life, and has a great deal of fun. The party she is arranging proves to be the turning point.

It's Me—Eileen

An office

Eileen and Deana are seated at their desks. It is coffee break in the morning, and they are sipping their coffee.
Deana bursts out laughing. It is infectious and Eileen joins in with her.

EILEEN Stop it, Deana! . . . You're mad! . . .

DEANA I know . . .

EILEEN What's so funny?

DEANA I didn't tell you what happened to me last night—or the early hours've this morning I should say . . . (*Deana giggles even louder.*)

EILEEN (*highly impatient*) Well tell me then!

DEANA Well, I had to walk home from some friends last night because I missed the last bus, and when I arrived I found I hadn't got my keys—I didn't know what to do—

EILEEN What about the girl you share the room with—couldn't she let you in?

DEANA   Oh her? She's left . . . And was I glad to see the back've that "Miss griz" . . . Anyway: my room's at the front of the house on the ground floor so I decided to try an' get in through the window—because I didn't want to have to wake the landlady—it was gone one! . . . You should've seen me, Eileen—it wasn't funny at the time . . . I climbed up onto the short wall by the stairs and split my skirt, stepped onto the ledge an' the heel've my shoe came off . . . I couldn't get the window open . . . I laddered my nylons an' I couldn't get back down again. There I was, clinging to the drain pipe for dear life—an' it started to rain! . . .

EILEEN   (*laughing at demonstration*) What happened?

DEANA   The landlady heard me an' thought I was a burglar so she phoned for the police! (*getting down with a flourish*) And they rescued me! . . .

EILEEN   (*admiringly*) You are mad, Deana, honestly . . .

DEANA   It was funny though . . .

They both move behind their desks.

DEANA   Hey! . . . have you decided yet whether or not you're coming to my birthday party tomorrow?

EILEEN   Yes. What time shall I come?

DEANA   Well, don't make it before nine-thirty, unless you want to help me prepare everything.

EILEEN   Nine-thirty!? . . . But I live about an hour's ride away from you and I have to be indoors by eleven . . .

DEANA   But it'll be Saturday—the crowd I mix with don't do anything or go anywhere until after nine . . .

EILEEN   It's not worth coming just for half an hour.

DEANA   Why don't you stay the night then? There's a spare bed now.

EILEEN   Are you kidding? My parents'd never stand for that.

DEANA   (*groans with mock horror*) Parents? . . . Don't mention them to me. What a drag . . . That problem's all in the past with me . . . Talk about not being able to lead your own life . . . They bring you into the world, and think that gives them the right to tell you exactly what you can and can't do . . . Demands! . . . Demands! . . . Demands! . . .

Eileen is silent and thoughtful. She finishes her coffee and recommences work.

The living room of Eileen's house

Early afternoon, the following Saturday. Eileen's mother is searching about the room for something.

MOTHER *(after searching along mantlepiece—calling off)* Eileen? . . . Eileen!

EILEEN *(heard off)* What?

MOTHER *(calling off)* What have you done with my butterfly brooch?!

EILEEN Nothing!

MOTHER *(calling)* You wore it last!

EILEEN *I* haven't got it!

Her mother crosses and starts to search sideboard.

MOTHER   (*calling off*) I asked you what you *did* with it!

EILEEN   I think it's on the sideboard!

MOTHER   (*calling off, exasperated*) It's not!!!

Eileen enters looking sullen and listless. She yawns.

MOTHER   (*laughing, amused*) Oh, you're up. Are we feeling refreshed now after our sixteen-hour little lie in?

EILEEN   (*grinning, in spite of herself*) Don't, Mum ... Listen, Why can't I stay at my friend's place?

MOTHER   I'm in a hurry, dear. Jimmy'll be here any minute and I'm not even ready.

EILEEN   (*slumping into settee*) But I *want* to, Mum.

MOTHER   (*laughs philosophically*) But we all "want to", love. (*Her hand is caught and she can't get it out from side of settee. She finds this funny.*) Oh, I've got me hand stuck.

EILEEN   Can I?—

MOTHER   Eileen, help me.

EILEEN   Ay, mum, can I?

MOTHER   Help me, Eileen!

Eileen crosses to her looking mischievous. She digs her mother in the ribs playfully.

EILEEN   Now can I? Ay? ...

MOTHER   Don't mess about, stop it.

EILEEN   Say "yes" then.

MOTHER   The time!

EILEEN   Can I?

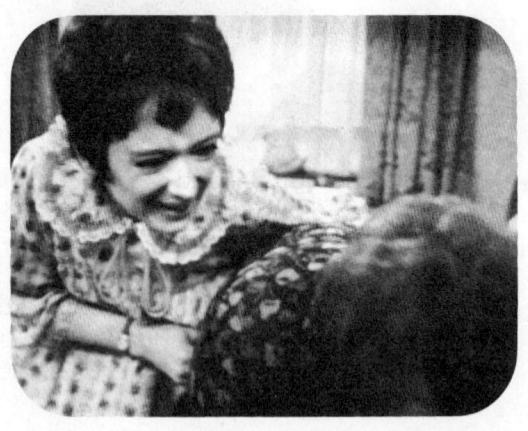

MOTHER Oh, am I going to get you, tomorrow morning, young lady . . .

EILEEN Will you promise not to pull the bedclothes off me first thing, darling?

MOTHER Only if you help me this instant.

Eileen assists her mother to free her hand by kneeling down on the side of the cushion and creating a gap. It's difficult as there is little room to move for both of them. They laugh and giggle.

MOTHER Mind my head!

EILEEN Move it then.

MOTHER How? by unscrewing it?

EILEEN No, take it off.

Her hand is free. She fishes about and brandishes the brooch.

MOTHER I knew it'd be down the side . . . (*she shakes her hand*) All the blood went out've it . . . Blinking thing! (*She kicks the settee.*)

EILEEN (*taking her hand and massaging it*) I don't think it'll swell . . .

MOTHER Even if I said you could—and I won't . . . Your father would never stand for you being out all night, Eileen.

EILEEN But it's *my* life!

There is a knock at the door.

MOTHER That'll be your brother and I'm not even ready yet. (*She goes out. Eileen sits down looking resentful.*)

EILEEN You might just as well talk to the wall . . . (*She slumps back on settee.*)

The hall passage

Eileen's mother lets Jimmy in. We see his fingers through the letter box fishing for the key that hangs from a string. Jimmy is about twenty-five, easy-going and likeable.

MOTHER   Hello, Jimmy, love.

(Jimmy kisses her on the cheek. Hugs her.)

JIMMY   Getcha coat on gal, Lena's waitin' in the car—we're late.

They walk towards the living room.

MOTHER   *(humorously)* I would've been ready but I got my hand caught down the side've the sofa—

JIMMY   Which one?

She shows her hand. He examines it and rubs it.

JIMMY   That'll teach you to go fishing for loose change—

She shoves him through the door, into

The living room

JIMMY   *(noticing Eileen's mood)* Hallo, sunshine! . . .

Crosses and chuffs her on the face, sparring playfully.

EILEEN   *(whacking his hand down)* Stop it!

JIMMY   Who's upset you?

EILEEN   No one!

Jimmy laughs as though to say "Not much". Eileen's mother tidying her hair at the mirror, turns to them.

MOTHER   She's in a mood because she can't stay the night at some friend's place . . . Talk to her, Jimmy.

EILEEN   *(leaps up indignantly)* That's it! "Talk to her"!

JIMMY   *(leaps back, mock fear)* Is that the girl you brought round to see us the other week?

EILEEN   Yes, it is.

JIMMY   *(to mother)* We gave her a lift home and the car broke down on the way back.

EILEEN   You can laugh, Jimmy, but you weren't timed with a blinking stop-watch before you were married! You did as you pleased!

MOTHER   She doesn't half lay it on thick.

JIMMY   I couldn't do as I pleased!

EILEEN As good as . . .

MOTHER She won't see it that parents worry more about a girl than a boy.

JIMMY I had to make sure Lena was back home at a certain time when we were courting.

EILEEN Oh, you don't understand . . . I can't do anything I want to!

MOTHER She's just got out of bed—two in the afternoon.

EILEEN What's there to get up for?

MOTHER What's there to get up for? When I was going out shop-

ping, she asked me to take her coat to the cleaners, get a
new battery for her radio, call into the supermarket and
tell her friend Joan she'd look in on her Monday night!
"What's there to get up for?" . . .

EILEEN That's not what I mean!

JIMMY What do you mean?

EILEEN Demands! . . . Do this, Eileen. Do that, Eileen. Go there
for me, Eileen.

MOTHER "Can I have my breakfast in bed, Mum? I won't be in
straight from the office tonight, Mum. Can you keep my
dinner in the oven?"
Jimmy looks from one to the other, amused.

EILEEN "Put a jumper over that blouse, Eileen, it might get cold!
Take your umbrella with you, Eileen, it might rain! Don't
wear those shoes, Eileen, you know they need repairing!"
Jimmy puts an arm round his mother's neck and pats her face.

JIMMY Well—the Duchess always made sure I didn't have odd
socks on before going out.

EILEEN Oh! . . . You never had to do housework . . . You just
floated in and out! . . .

MOTHER You little spitfire you! (*To Jimmy*) I made her stay in Tuesday and Thursday night last week. She was out the other

nights . . . She's even given her boyfriend the cold shoulder . . . He was round each night, poor devil . . . "Is Eileen in, please? Will you tell her I want to see her, please?"

EILEEN He's another one—all demands—my life's not my own! . . . I mustn't dance with another fellah. Because he wants to go serious, I've got to!

MOTHER You haven't got to. He loves you. Be nice to him. He's having a hard time of it, that's what you do to him . . . Let him down gently . . . If the boys weren't interested in you, you'd soon be wishing you had a few demands being made . . .

EILEEN Hah! . . . He doesn't concern himself with me when he's got other things to do.

MOTHER Oh we've had a row, have we?

EILEEN What's the point of trying to say something! No one listening.

MOTHER Let's be serious for a minute, Eileen. (*Eileen is about to register a further protest.*) No, I mean really serious. Do you want to come with us to your Uncle John's?

EILEEN No, thanks . . . I'm going to my friend's party.

MOTHER All right, but make sure you're in by midnight . . .

They go into the hall passage

MOTHER There you are—I'm giving you an extra hour.

EILEEN (*loudly*) The party doesn't start till late! (*She goes into her bedroom.*)
Her mother is leaning against the wall, laughing helplessly and silently. Jimmy grins ruefully.

MOTHER (*sotto voce*) What would you do with her . . . ?
Jimmy opens the front door.

MOTHER (*calling out*) Have a quick tidy up before you go out will you, Eileen? Only your father'll be in before I get back!
They hurry out.

EILEEN (*heard off at the top of her voice*) Demands! Demands! Demands!!

77

Deana's bed-sitter

Eileen enters carrying a coat and a couple of dresses.

DEANA Well, this is it.

EILEEN It's nice, isn't it.

DEANA Put your coat across that chair for now . . .
Eileen does so and looks about her.

DEANA This is your bed.
Eileen crosses to the bed

DEANA I hope you're going to like it here, Eileen.

EILEEN (*nods enthusiastically*) It's so . . . so . . . well it's . . . Oh I can't describe what I feel!
They laugh together.

DEANA I like the doll.
She takes it and puts it on mantlepiece.

EILEEN It was my grandmother's, then my mother's, and then mine.
Eileen starts to stack her things on her bed. Deana crosses back to Eileen, then to chest of drawers, with cola tins

DEANA I can't wait for tonight to come . . .

EILEEN Roll on tonight!
They laugh together.

DEANA (*By chest of drawers, opening one*) These two top ones are yours, and this small one on the right—(*crossing to sink*) but don't put your things in yet until I've lined them with some fresh paper.

Eileen had started to move towards drawers. Deana crosses to the mantlepiece with bottles.

EILEEN Shall I help you with them?

DEANA I can't tell you how pleased I am to have you here . . . I've dreaded coming back to this room every night from the office, to be greeted by a deafening silence—from no one! . . . I thought I'd end up talking to myself . . . (*Eileen laughs as Deana crackles on*) You'd be surprised the noises a room makes in the middle of the night when you're on your own . . . Talk about "snap, crackle, and pop"! Couple of times I thought the floor boards were moving! Peculiar noises, I'm not kidding! I was so scared I could hardly breathe! And my heart! . . . (*Pounds her chest and knocks her head from side to side, eyes wide in rolling*) Boom, boom, boom, gawk! (*Eileen finds her highly amusing. Deana continues more subdued*) D'you know what, Eileen?

EILEEN What?

DEANA A couple of nights when I went out last week I put about eight LP's on the player and switched them on before leaving, so as there'd be music on when I came in and I could pretend someone was here . . . Daft, en it?

EILEEN No, it's a good idea . . .

DEANA Anyway, I won't have to do that again. (*Deana goes to kitchen and back. As she comes back she notices Eileen looking thoughtful.*) You're quiet all of a sudden.

EILEEN I'm just thinking.

DEANA What?

EILEEN How nice it is here.

DEANA Oh . . . I thought perhaps you were having second thoughts about coming . . . But didn't want to say.

EILEEN (*laughs*) Of course not.

DEANA I'm sorry the place is upside-down. I just haven't been able to face it.

EILEEN I like it all topsy turvy. Still I suppose we ought to tidy up for the party.

Eileen gets up to start clearing up.

DEANA   No, you won't! Old "Miss Griz" hardly did a thing . . .
        Did she get on my nerves! . . . Have you known people
        like that? . . . Everything they do irritates you . . .
EILEEN Not really . . . Didn't you know the girl before she came?
DEANA   (*laughs, surprised*) Of course! We used to go out a lot with
        two brothers . . . But when she came here and I really got
        to know her! . . .
EILEEN (*crossing to her case*) I hope you'll still like me this time next
        week.
DEANA   I'm bound to, look how well we get on together at work.
        (*Surveys room, hands on hips*) Now, where shall I start first?
        Yes, the beds.

        *Deana crosses to Eileen's bed and places case on floor, taking it
        out of Eileen's hand. She whips the cover and blanket off, then
        the sheets.*
        Eileen takes one end of them.
EILEEN I'll make my bed. (*tugging blankets.*)
DEANA   (*also tugging blankets*) Oh, no you won't!
EILEEN (*tugging harder*) I will!
DEANA   (*tugs back harder*) You won't!
        Eileen falls on the bed. They both giggle.
DEANA   It's your first day here and you didn't make the mess, so
        sit down and watch me.

Eileen then notices dirty dishes in bowl and crosses to wash them. Deana turns and sees her:

DEANA   (*in a pleasant bossy way*) Leave it, Eileen. I've told you I'll see to everything.

EILEEN   But I want to do something!

DEANA   Don't be silly, you don't!

EILEEN   But I do!

Deana, adopting a mock matronly manner, crosses to her, and dumps her in a chair.

DEANA   Have a read. (*Eileen flicks the pages of the magazine while Deana makes the bed.*) D'you fancy a fry-up? I have fry-ups all the time.

EILEEN   Do you?

The living room of Eileen's home

Father enters with a tea tray and sits on the sofa. Mother enters a little after.

MOTHER   Hello, love, been in long?

FATHER   About an hour.

MOTHER   Did you make yourself some tea?

He shakes his head. She crosses to sideboard and places her hand-bag down, then she notices Eileen's key on end of a charm ring.

MOTHER   Oh, that girl!

FATHER What's she done now?

MOTHER Gone out and left her key behind. (*taking off coat*) That means one've us 'll have to get up and let her in. (*Her husband looks across sharply.*) I said she could stay out until midnight because it's her friend's birthday and she's having a party . . .

She lays her coat on the settee and sits down.

MOTHER (*laughs reflectively*) Oh, she was funny this afternoon, Ted . . . You should've seen her . . . She pestered me and pestered me to let her stay there all night—

FATHER (*looking up quickly*) Stay where?

MOTHER At her friend's place! I've just told you! I'm sure you don't listen to half the things I say! . . . Oh but she was funny! . . . Jimmy was here as well. We laughed . . . She's a whirlwind when she starts, that one. (*Rises and crosses to leave the room*) No getting away from it . . . I don't know which one've us she takes after.

FATHER (*looking up again*) Don't you?

MOTHER I was never like that as a youngster!

FATHER (*moving away with a sour expression*) Not much!

MOTHER (*laughs, pleased*) Got away with you! . . .

The bed-sitter in the early evening

The two girls are seated with their meals on laps.

DEANA You're quiet.

EILEEN Just thinking.

DEANA What about?

EILEEN Isn't it nice here?

DEANA By the way, hang onto your sixpences and shillings. They come in handy for the meter when you want a bath . . . And for the fire and cooker in here . . .

EILEEN How do you work out whose turn it is to put money into the meter for the fire and cooker?

DEANA Oh, just take it in turns, you know.

EILEEN Yes, but how do you check whose turn it is?

DEANA I've never bothered about it really.

EILEEN This is like camping.

DEANA Yes.

Eileen notices that Deana is on edge. She puts her meal down and crosses to her handbag. Takes out a small package, crosses and hands it to Deana.

EILEEN Many happy returns . . .

DEANA What is it?

EILEEN (*sitting again*) Only something cheap.

DEANA (*opening it*) You shouldn't've.

EILEEN Why not?

DEANA   Thanks very much. What did your mother say when you told her you were leaving?
Eileen shakes her head.

DEANA   (*laughing*) Please yourself what you do? . . .
Eileen smiles diplomatically, then looks thoughtful.

The living room that same evening

Eileen's mother tidies her hair and checks her make-up. Her husband brushes his cap and settles it on his head. They are about to go to the local for a Saturday night drink.

MOTHER   Where'd you get the idea that I was like Eileen as a youngster?

FATHER   I've got a very good memory.

MOTHER   I never had the freedom she has and even if I'd had it, I could never've earned the kind of money she does to enjoy it . . .

FATHER   I was thinking about your antics then, and hers now.

MOTHER   Listen to you—

FATHER   Come on. The pubs'll be closed if we hang around here much longer—get your coat.

MOTHER   I'm just going into Eileen's room, I want to borrow one of her scarves. Your shirt collar's all twisted up at the back.

	She goes out, leaving the father muttering.
MOTHER	*(heard from off)* Oh, Ted!
FATHER	Yes.
	Mother re-enters quickly.
MOTHER	It's Eileen! Her things are gone!
FATHER	*(looks at her, uncomprehending)* What?

MOTHER	Her things—her clothes.
FATHER	What d'you mean, someone's broken in?
MOTHER	I mean she's packed her clothes in a case and left.
FATHER	She can't have left.
MOTHER	But she has.
FATHER	Why! She can't have left over nothing.
MOTHER	I can't understand it. I was only teasing her.
FATHER	What's been happening between you two?
MOTHER	She started to play up because I wouldn't let her stay out the night—I joked a bit about it. She took it well enough. At least I thought she did . . .
FATHER	It looks like it. *(he crosses to the door)* Oh! I'd better get round to the police station.
MOTHER	No, don't do that—Go round to Jimmy's.
FATHER	In it marvellous, ay! *All* day I've been looking forward to a drink and this happens.

Deana's bed-sitter later that night

There is a gramophone playing, and Deana is being bumped.

GROUP   Fourteen, fifteen, sixteen, seventeen . . .

Everyone cheers. The camera holds Deana as she is put down. She goes and sits on Eileen's bed with girls. Pete goes to pull her up again. Turns to crowd.

PETE   Can I have your attention everyone? . . . Put that record off someone, will you please?

A boy takes the record off.

PETE This is more than just a party! This is Deana's birthday party! (*We see Deana's reaction.*) I've got something special for you.

DEANA A present?

PETE Better than a present . . . I'm going to sing to you!
They all follow Pete in singing "Happy Birthday to You" loudly and boisterously.
Deana suddenly rushes out of the room. They all look at each other perplexed. There is hubbub.

EILEEN Don't let her catch us all staring at her when she comes back in!

PETE Put the record back on, someone! (*Someone does, and the music starts.*) Dance everyone.

The dancing starts, but in a subdued mood. Cut to two girls by the door.

ANGELA She's crying her heart out in the bathroom, and we can't get in because she's locked the door and won't open it.

Eileen hurries out of the room. While she is out we see shots of couples dancing in the small room. Eileen comes back. All look at her expectantly.

EILEEN I'm sorry but I think everyone had better go because she's a bit upset.

BILLY What's the matter with her?

EILEEN I don't know.

PETE Is she all right?

EILEEN I think so . . . She's just upset about something—she's not ill.

While we see a close up of Eileen looking anxious, we hear cries of disappointment as they start to collect their coats from the bed, and remarks: "Just warming up".

The living room of Eileen's home a little later

MOTHER What are we going to do, Jimmy?

FATHER Go to the police.

JIMMY (*stopping him*) Just a minute, dad.

MOTHER I don't know how she could do this to me . . . I mean what have I done?

FATHER You've let her have too much of her own way!

MOTHER I haven't!

FATHER She winds you round her little finger!

MOTHER And what about you? . . . You don't spoil her, I suppose!

JIMMY Mum!

FATHER No, I don't!

JIMMY Dad!

MOTHER I can't understand what reason she's got for doing it.

JIMMY Don't argue amongst yourselves . . .

Dad crosses to the door.

MOTHER What are you going now?

FATHER I'm going to the police!

MOTHER You stay here and let Jimmy go. Go on Jimmy, you go.

FATHER I'll go with him.

MOTHER No. You'll only start shouting the odds.

JIMMY Stay with mum, dad . . . I won't be long . . .

Jimmy exits.

MOTHER (*to herself, aloud*) Oh . . . I don't know I'm sure . . . That

89

girl . . . The worry . . . Maybe it's my fault . . . I do laugh at her when she sounds off, and I suppose I shouldn't . . . I don't know I'm sure . . .

The bed-sitter

The room is now left to Eileen again. We see Deana sitting quietly by the fire.

EILEEN (*heard from the other side of the room*) What's the matter, Deana? (*but Deana does not seem to hear*) Can't you tell me? (*There's no answer.*) Can't you? . . . Deana? . . . Can't you tell me? You'll feel much better if you do . . . At least get into bed.

DEANA Oh, leave me alone.
Eileen thinks about this and then goes to the chest of drawers to start to pack. Deana watches her for a while.

DEANA What are you doing, Eileen?

EILEEN What's it look like?

DEANA Look, I'm sorry. (*There's no reply*) I didn't mean it like that. I'd rather you stayed. Don't go. (*But the packing goes on.*) I'm sorry about tonight, but it's nothing to do with you.

EILEEN What is it then?

DEANA Oh, it's all daft. Do you know what started it? A bloody card. (*Eileen looks at her.*) Yes, a birthday card. I didn't get one from me parents.

EILEEN   Well, perhaps they forgot.

DEANA   They didn't forget. They just don't care. We had this row, you see, before I left. I had to go, but I've written to them several times. No answer. It's gone on for months. You kid yourself it doesn't matter but it does. It's funny. Maybe it don't worry you. You can get on without them perhaps.

EILEEN   Mine are not the same.

There is a pause.

DEANA   Are you still going?

EILEEN   I ought to.

DEANA   I don't like being on my own tonight. (*Eileen doesn't know what to do.*) I'm very lonely, really. You'd be good for me. *We see Eileen's reaction in close up, and then there is a knock at the door. It opens as Jimmy enters.*

EILEEN   Hello, Jimmy?

JIMMY   I remembered the house . . . I thought there'd be loud music coming from the room. The party's over early isn't it?

EILEEN   It's only just ended . . .

Jimmy nods to Deana, who smiles ill at ease. He notices Eileen's case.

JIMMY   I'm supposed to be at the police station now reporting that you're missing . . . There's no need for that now . . . But I'll have to tell the folks I've seen you . . . And you know that means they'll be round like greased lightn-

ing . . . What're you going to do? (*Eileen is in a quandary.*,
Well, if you're open to suggestions I thought you could stay
at my place tonight . . . Talk it over with Lena . . . I'll tell
mum you're with us . . . And then she can come round in
the morning and you can say your piece there . . . (*There
is a considerable pause. After a while he rises.*) Well, how about
it?
*We see first a close up of Deana and then Eileen as the play
ends.*

Clean Sweep

by Ronald Eyre

The Cast

The Narrator

Mr Collett, *Managing Director and Owner*
Mr Thomas, *a manager*

Gregg, *a new apprentice*
Hesketh, *an older apprentice*
Mr Glassford, *a foreman*
Another foreman

Watson,
First man
Second man } *workers in the pressing shop*
Third man

Miss Carey, *Mr Collett's secretary*
Tea girl

Collett's Works seems a small factory like any other. But this factory, and the people in it, had settled into a habit-ridden routine in which everyone knew what was expected and what could be got away with. In some ways this was comfortable, though it allowed domineering men, like Watson in the pressing shop, to run their own little empires and make life uncomfortable for those who wouldn't fit. Now, though, it looks as if there's going to be a clean sweep.

Clean Sweep

The outer office of Collett's Works

Workmen are shifting old desks and shelves under the eye of young Mr Collett, age about thirty-two and pushy. He is accompanied by Mr Thomas, a man who looks older than his years and carries a note pad.

NARRATOR Young Mr Collett of Collett's Works, Filey Street, had often said: "I wish I could get my hands on this place. I'd make a clean sweep." When old Mr Collett retired, young Mr Collett took over and the clean sweep began.

Collett and Thomas have gone through into Collett's office.

Mr Collett's office

There are big dark shelves round the room. Portraits of father and grandfather and imposing groups of directors.

Collett is giving a brisk series of orders to Mr Thomas. Through the open door can be seen the general office, Collett's brisk young secretary at her desk, and the men working.

THOMAS All these cupboards?

COLLETT Clean sweep.

THOMAS (*writing*) All mahogany to go.

COLLETT Walls white, fitted shelves—that wall and that wall. Fitted carpets.

THOMAS To match the rugs?

COLLETT No. There won't be any rugs. (*Thomas winces and tries to hide his reaction.*) Venetian blinds. White. (*Presses intercom switch.*) Miss Carey.

SECRETARY'S
VOICE (*heard distorted*) Yes, sir.

COLLETT Furnishing fabrics. A book or two of samples. Trendy. Pronto. All right?

SECRETARY Yes, sir. (*Collett takes his finger from the switch.*)

THOMAS   A wonderful device sir. The intercommunicating radio.

COLLETT   (*withering*) Yes, Mr Thomas. These days we call it the intercom.

THOMAS   Ah.

COLLETT   Or better still—nothing.

THOMAS   Yes, sir.

COLLETT   (*hesitating*) Mr Thomas. (*Thomas braces himself to hear the worst.*) When did you last buy a suit?

THOMAS   A suit sir? Er. 1963 the last one sir. Yes, 1963. That's for best of course. This (*indicating his suit*) I'm proud to say belongs to the late 50's and it's a living proof that with a bit of patient swabbing and a flat iron there's nothing to beat the craftsmanship of yesterday. Nothing. Not of course that I'm against change. Far from it. Your father retires, you take his place. New ideas. All of them quite excellent. (*He is trying to get through to young Collett.*) And if I appear a little shocked as this or that part of my life's work gets . . . er . . . removed . . . , I hope you'll understand that it takes a little time to adjust. Not of course that I offer resistance . . . I don't.

Intercom buzzes. Collett answers it.

COLLETT   Yes, Miss Carey.

MISS CAREY   Watson from the pressing shop to see Mr Thomas. New boy Gregg waiting for interview.

COLLETT   Thank you, Miss Carey. That's all then, Mr Thomas.

THOMAS   Yes, sir. (*He starts to withdraw then stops.*) Just to make sure, sir. Not wanting to make an error. I can hold out no hope to Watson?

COLLETT   Not automatic hope, no. There's nothing automatic in this factory except machinery and the intercom. Promotion comes to those who deserve it. It is a reward, not a right.

THOMAS   I understand, sir.

COLLETT   Good.

THOMAS   So I'll see Watson and tell him. (*Affecting indignation.*) He can't expect to be a charge-hand just because of his seniority.

COLLETT   That's right, Thomas. You tell him.

THOMAS   Yes, sir. And the new boy.

COLLETT Let the new boy see the new boy eh?

         He smiles emptily and slaps Thomas on the shoulder. Thomas
         exits. Collett's face drops.

Outer office

Mr Thomas looks like a man under sentence of death.

MISS CAREY You can go in now.

         Gregg, sixteen years old, serious, tough, stands up and goes into
         the office.

THOMAS   (*smiles at Miss Carey*) Awfully impressive, Mr Christopher,
         though I shouldn't like him to know I said so. (*He goes.*)

Mr Collett's office

Collett is at his desk. Before him sits Gregg.

COLLETT Yes. That's how he got them to march. "Every soldier," he
         said, "carries in his knapsack a field marshal's baton."
         Incentive, you see. Feed ambition, create comradeship.
         All proper things to do. And he started in Corsica. An
         underprivileged lad. We can't all be Napoleons, Gregg.
         But there's a future for the right lad with a right attitude to
         the firm, to me personally, to his foreman, his teachers—
         on day release.

GREGG   Yes, sir.

         The door opens and Mr Thomas puts his head in.

THOMAS   It's not being altogether easy, sir. (*Sees Gregg*) Oh, sorry.

COLLETT (*frostily*) That's all right, Thomas.

         Thomas retreats fast. Collett glances at Gregg.

COLLETT Mr Thomas!

THOMAS   (*in again*) Yes, sir?

COLLETT We shall be about thirty seconds.

THOMAS   Yes, sir (*withdraws*).

COLLETT (*to Gregg*) Another generation. They don't understand.
         (*He pushes intercom switch.*) So you'll start Monday morning
         in the pressing shop. Very much as Napoleon started in
         Corsica. And we all know where he finished.

GREGG   Yes, sir. St Helena, sir.

COLLETT   You're a bright boy Gregg, but he had a hell of a time before he got there, didn't he? That's all, Gregg. (*Gregg rises and leaves.*)

COLLETT   (*pushes down intercom switch*) Mr Thomas, Miss Carey.

MISS CAREY   (*distorted*) He went back to his office, sir.

COLLETT   (*looking frustrated*) Hm.

Outer office

Miss Carey switches off the intercom. Miss Carey looks up with a smile at Gregg.

MISS CAREY   Now Mr . . . Gregg. We've had your report cards from the Technical College photostated so would you return them with thanks to the Principal's secretary.

GREGG   (*taking them*) Thanks.

MISS CAREY   I hope you'll be very happy here. (*She smiles at him.*)

Mr Collett's office

Mr Collett drops the latch on his door and switches on a special switch on his intercom. He can hear what is happening.

Mr Thomas's office

It is still furnished in the old style. Watson is sitting looking miserable. He is aged about forty-three, strongly built, and now wears a woebegone expression.

WATSON   It's the injustice, Mr Thomas. I was sixteen when I came here. I've given service, haven't I? Twenty years is service. What's he got against me?

THOMAS   Nothing. Oh nothing. And twenty years *is* twenty years.

WATSON   Not when you've nothing to show for it.

THOMAS   Now, Watson. Try and be moderate.

WATSON   Moderate? Would you be moderate if you'd bought on the H.P. knowing to the penny what you'd be worth when your seniority came up? Only to find out that it hasn't? What do I do with a four berth caravan? Do you want it?

THOMAS	No thank you, Watson.
WATSON	No, you don't. Am I a criminal? Just answer me that, am I a criminal?
THOMAS	Of course not.
WATSON	Then why am I not fit to be a charge-hand?
THOMAS	It's not that you're not fit, Watson. You probably are. (*Watson looks at him.*) You *certainly* are. But your twenty years don't automatically make you fit. That's the new rule.
WATSON	What? You mean we have to get us O-levels.
THOMAS	I don't know. Really I don't. I'm used to the old ways too you know, Watson. There was neatness before. Everybody had the same expectations. Change may be necessary, Watson, but don't ask me to defend it. I am here just to say—changes are to be. It's a set back. You are a victim. What more can I do?
WATSON	Twenty blasted years, twenty blasted years.

Mr Collett's office

Collett who has been seen listening at crucial points in the conversation switches off his intercom.

The pressing shop

NARRATOR	The following Monday Gregg came to work.
	During the Narrator's words Gregg comes in and looks at Watson and walks past him. Hesketh is working further away.
WATSON	Looking for something?
GREGG	The pressing shop.
WATSON	Well, stop looking. You've arrived.
GREGG	Is this the pressing shop?
WATSON	The very same. What can I do for you?
GREGG	Aren't you expecting me?
WATSON	No. Did you expect us to be?
GREGG	I'm working here. New learner. Mr Collett saw me.
WATSON	There's only enough useful work here for one learner and we've got one. I reckon they've sent you to the wrong shop. So don't get set in.

GREGG   You said this was the pressing shop. Is it the only pres-
         sing shop?

WATSON   Yes, it is and you're not expected. Stand out of the way a
         minute. (*To Hesketh*) Keep him out of mischief. Tiny, keep
         him out of mischief.

         Watson goes. Hesketh comes over to Gregg.

HESKETH You new then?

GREGG   Yes.

HESKETH What's your name?

GREGG   Gregg.

HESKETH First day, is it . . . I bet it is . . . Ah they'll have it in for you.

GREGG   Who will?

HESKETH Everybody. It starts like that. You'll have your leg pulled.
         Don't let it worry you though. We've all had to go through
         it.

GREGG   Sounds like a proper waste of time to me. How long do
         they carry on?

HESKETH Not long. Don't worry. It gets better after that. Pity you
         won't be in this section.

GREGG   Why?

HESKETH We have a cushy time. My uncle Harry, that's the one who
         just went. He's my mother's brother so he's called Watson.
         He's got it as comfy as a foam-rubber mattress. He's in
         charge really. There's a foreman but nobody takes any
         notice. It's Watson's shop if it's anybody's, and you
         should see what he makes on the side. He ought to be a
         charge-hand really, but there's a new rule out. Play it his
         way and you can't go wrong.

NARRATOR And while they talk, Watson is with Mr Glassford in his
         office.

The foreman's cubicle:

*The foreman's cubicle has "Mr Glassford" on the door. Inside
Watson and Glassford are talking. Watson treats Glassford with
real scorn, though he veils it.*

WATSON   It can slip anybody's mind or get lost. A bit of paper.
         (*Glassford is searching.*) Perhaps you never had it.

GLASSFORD   Oh, yes I did. A note to say a new lad would be arriving and to put him in the pressing shop . . . I had it only yesterday.

WATSON   (*appearing to try and help*) Try your turn-ups, Mr Glassford. (*Glassford looks at him.*) No really . . . lots of things . . .

GLASSFORD   Anyway you say he's arrived and I say he's expected. So that's that.

WATSON   But it's not as easy as that, Mr Glassford. There's room for one learner and we've got one. We can't use a second, and young Brian's doing all right. It's a good team you've got there, Mr Glassford.

GLASSFORD   And don't I know it?

WATSON   I can tell you on sight that this new lad won't make a contribution. It's a case of the management not being in touch.

GLASSFORD   Well the management want him and it's their right you know, Watson. So there you are. It's up to you. His name's . . . (*he can't think*).

WATSON   I'll ask him.

GLASSFORD   And he's got a good report from the Tech. The new Mr Collett is insisting on that for all the new entrants. This firm's out to attract a better type of lad.

WATSON   So *we'll* have to watch our p's and q's. Won't we, Mr Glassford?

GLASSFORD   I'll be along to see he's getting the right treatment from you, Watson.

WATSON   Understood, Mr Glassford.

As Watson is seen going back to the shop, we hear the narrator.

NARRATOR   So Gregg started work in the pressing shop and he learned fast. But apart from the job he had two sets of rules to learn. Factory rules and Watson's rules. Because, as everybody knew, the pressing shop was Watson's corner.

The factory floor

A tea bell. The men stop working and queue at the tea trolley. Gregg goes on working.

FIRST MAN	And once he started pulling he couldn't stop. And it stretched $2\frac{1}{2}$ feet. All out of one sausage roll.
SECOND MAN	Give it a rest.
FIRST MAN	It's the truth. Jab a fork in it and it'll swear back at you.
THIRD MAN	Take him a cup of tea, Sam.
WATSON	A cup of tea? He wants an 'earing aid. Didn't you hear that bell ring?
GREGG	What bell?
WATSON	That work bell.
GREGG	'Course I did. I'm not deaf.
WATSON	Well, that bell means lay off or else your tea'll get cold. And we don't keep it under a cosy.
GREGG	I'm just finishing off.
WATSON	Listen. You don't finish off. You stop. There's lots of time later for finishing off. Too much time.
GREGG	But I'd have to go back to the beginning if I left off now.
WATSON	Well, go back to the beginning. What do you think the rest of the day's for? I can see you've got to learn your ABC yet. There's factory rules and there's our rules, and while you're in this shop our rules go. And our rules are simple:
	1 We pull together when things are O.K.
	2 We stand by one another when they're not.
	3 We don't kill ourselves for £20 a week.
GREGG	You can say that again.
WATSON	They're our rules. And while you're here, you keep them.
NARRATOR	Gregg and Watson—two natural enemies because they are alike. Soon it's open warfare.

The factory floor again later

Gregg's slide rule has been hidden.

GREGG	Did you see my slide rule? What have you done with it?
WATSON	What have I done with what?
GREGG	You know.
WATSON	I don't know. What's eating you? If you go on like that you'll end up with ulcers.

GREGG   I left my slide rule on this box. You took it.

WATSON   I took it? Look here, Cocky, be careful who you accuse. You can get into hot water for making false accusations. Get all the facts before you let rip.

GREGG   Well, I'll have it back anyway.

WATSON   Sit down. Your tea'll be getting cold.

GREGG   Let it.

WATSON   He's never at a loss for words, is he? Our new lad. He knows what he wants. He's got a mind of his own. And he's ambitious. Aren't you? Ambitious? Given half a chance he'd be here all hours of the day and night. So long as it got noticed. Wouldn't you, Gregg? Put on quite a show if you knew the boss'd see it? (*Gregg is still searching.*) Anyway you can lay off searching . . . (*throws some money on the table*) I'll have ten fags. Little shop outside the gates. First left, then left again. Woman who runs it called Avril. Be nice to her.

GREGG   Me?

WATSON   Yes, you. You've got ten minutes to be there and back. I'm dying for a smoke.

GREGG   Well, die then.

WATSON   Gregg. Believe me. Somebody's going to teach you your place.

GREGG   I was told my place when I started, and it's not running errands for you.
There is a silence.

HESKETH   (*producing the slide rule, apparently from Gregg's lunch tin*) What's this here then?

WATSON   It's a device for measuring coppers' feet. (*He laughs. Gregg lunges at it.*) Steady on. You'll do yourself a serious injury. (*Gregg still trying to get it.*) Brawn as well as brain. See if you can clear that. (*Holding the ruler in an awkward position over a bench.*) Come on, you can do most other things. Don't give in. Put your back into it. (*Gregg sits down.*) Now don't tell me you're giving up. Where's the cheeky answer? Why not the usual backchat? What's happening to you? (*To the others*) He's going to get on, this one, you know. He's the sort they like.

HESKETH	*(going up to Gregg with the slide rule)* What do you do with this thing anyway?
GREGG	You wouldn't understand. So don't strain yourself.
WATSON	You'd better watch out or they'll be giving you your gold watch for your fifty years and then what'll you have to look forward to? You're too clever by half.
HESKETH	Shall I get your fags, Uncle Harry?
WATSON	You'd better. His lordship doesn't feel inclined.
HESKETH	Would it be O.K. to go now?
WATSON	Keep your eyes open. You're all right. Make sure this chap with the slide rule doesn't see you, though. Else the boss'll know in no time. *(To Gregg)* Like to slip off and tell him? Hesketh's taking ten minutes off to do me a favour.
GREGG	Why should *I* tell him? He most likely knows already. *The reaction of the other men is to laugh at Watson. As we see them going back to their work—*
NARRATOR	The weeks pass. For the first time in his fifteen years Watson has met his match.

Mr Collet's office

COLLETT	Which all adds up to something very pleasant, Gregg. They like you at the Tech and you're doing well here.
GREGG	Thank you, sir.
COLLETT	So you can expect to be in the pressing shop for a month or two more and then we'll give you a change. Is that all right?
GREGG	Yes, sir.
COLLETT	No complaints?
GREGG	No complaints, sir.
COLLETT	Smoke?
GREGG	No, I don't, thanks.
COLLETT	Neither do I. Now you, like all the others, keep your mouth shut when someone in an office asks about what happens on the factory floor. And that's just how it should be. We respect your loyalty to the team. But there is another sort of loyalty, of course. Your loyalty to the firm. Which means no more than this really, that when I choose

to have a talk with you like this I can feel that you can trust me and that I can trust you and that neither of us will leave this room and talk about what we say within it. We respect each other in this sense. Do you understand?

GREGG Yes, sir.

COLLETT Good.

Mr Glassford's office

GLASSFORD So Watson, take a look at it. Target 9,000. Output 8,552. You're 448 behind, Watson.

WATSON I know, Mr Glassford. I can do arithmetic as well.

GLASSFORD Have you any explanation then? You've a man extra, with Gregg . . . And, before you start, don't bother to wrap it up. Just give me the reason straight.

WATSON You've just given the reason yourself. The extra man. He's got to be shown everything. That slows things up.

GLASSFORD For a bit it does, but once he's shown, they can get faster. You've got to do better than that.

WATSON They would if it were anybody else but Gregg. He slows things up.

GLASSFORD Gregg?

WATSON You've no idea, Mr Glassford.

GLASSFORD But he's a bright lad. They've got their eye on him upstairs.

WATSON Bright? You must be mixing him up. He tries, but he hasn't got it. He's uncoordinated. I've watched him. He'll never be a patch on our Brian, certificates and all. Our Brian can run rings round him. You can't get everything down on a certificate, you know. I don't doubt there's lots of jobs he'd fit in. But not in this section. And I hope for his own sake he realises before long. You can be very unhappy in the wrong job.

GLASSFORD I know all that. And when I want your advice I'll ask for it.

WATSON Sorry.

There's a knock on the door. Glassford says "Come in". Gregg enters. There's an awkward pause as Gregg sees Watson.

GLASSFORD It's past your hometime, isn't it lad?

GREGG Yes, Mr Glassford. I wonder if I could have the key to No. 17 locker. I left my bag in there and Hesketh locked it when he went off.

GLASSFORD Well, why don't you take your bag out at the proper time? When everybody was going off?

GREGG I wasn't there at the proper time. I've been off since tea break.

GLASSFORD What do you mean? Off since tea break?

GREGG I was called away. Mr Collett wanted to see me.

GLASSFORD Mr Collett? You've been with Mr Collett since tea break?

GREGG Me and a few others. He saw some of the learners as well. It wasn't anything.

The key is handed over.

GLASSFORD No. 17. Hurry back. We're closing. (*When he has gone Glassford looks uneasy.*) He might have sent me a bit of paper, Mr Collett might. To tell me he wanted to see Gregg specially.

WATSON He might. But you might have lost it.

NARRATOR And Watson wonders what Gregg has said to Mr Collett. A few weeks go by. Mr Glassford keeps himself to himself and doesn't tread on Watson's toes. But one day his hand is forced.

We see another foreman talking through the glass door.

FOREMAN Can I see you a minute, Bill?

The pressing shop

The men are at work. Glassford and the other foreman come down and walk across the floor.

GLASSFORD Did you see him?

FOREMAN It wasn't any of these. But I know he's from this section. There were two lads. One had a frightened face and lot of hair. The other was a thick-set type, a bit serious looking.

GLASSFORD That would be Gregg.

FOREMAN The serious one?

GLASSFORD Yes.

FOREMAN He'd be the one I asked. He was collecting some material from the H.S.F. stores and I told him to hurry else I'd lock him in. So he said he'd only be five minutes but he didn't know about his pal. "Where's your pal?" I said. "Let's have a look at him." And the lad said "Other side of those boxes." I went to the other side of the shelves and there was this lad as large as life, a freckly lad, dragging away at a cigarette like the factory chimney. I got him by the scruff of the neck and punched him out into the yard. One spark from that and the whole factory would be ablaze. Can you credit it? Kids! Anyway he's one of yours. Although I can't see him anywhere.

GLASSFORD (*looking miserable*) Yes. He's one of mine. It'd be Hesketh. Did you say freckles?

FOREMAN Yes, freckles.

GLASSFORD Hesketh.

FOREMAN Well no doubt he knows what's coming to him. Are you going to report it or shall I?

GLASSFORD Yes. It's all right. Leave him to me. I'll telephone right away. Now I know who it was.

We leave Glassford and the foreman and cut to another part of the shop.

WATSON Gregg!

FIRST MAN Hesketh was on the other side of the boxes from Gregg. I saw it happen.

WATSON You mean to tell me Gregg didn't know Hesketh was having a smoke? Gregg? Course he did. I wouldn't put it past Gregg to suggest it to him.

SECOND MAN Hesketh's that easily influenced.

WATSON He's only a lad.

THIRD MAN Don't worry, Harry. Glassford won't telephone the works manager.

WATSON He'd better not.

FIRST MAN Glassford'll find a way round it. Anything for a quiet life.

Glassford approaches the phone.

THIRD MAN Glassford's picked up the phone.

SECOND MAN It's going through to the management.

As Glassford is seen talking on the phone, the men freeze, and we hear the Narrator's voice.

NARRATOR The men see Glassford on the phone. But what they don't see is his finger on the button. So that, although he puts in a full report about Hesketh, nobody receives it, anything for a quiet life. (*During this we see, close, Glassford's finger on the button and his mouth talking.*) But as far as the men are concerned the complaint has gone through. And Hesketh is for it. As indeed he is. But not as he expects.

Mr Collett's office

COLLETT After a report like this Hesketh must certainly give up his learnership.

THOMAS But sir, there's many a lad not academically gifted who's an asset to the shop floor.

COLLETT Tripe. Achievement is achievement. If he can't satisfy the Tech., he can't satisfy us. In the new Collett and Son we are technologists.

THOMAS Yes, sir. Shall I tell him, sir?

COLLETT You send for him. I'll tell him. That will impress him. Yes?

The factory floor

Hesketh and Watson near the lockers. Hesketh opens one and starts taking his stuff out.

NARRATOR And on the factory floor Gregg is sent to Coventry.

WATSON We had one of his type a couple of years ago. He lasted all of three weeks and that showed remarkable endurance.

GREGG (*to Hesketh*) What are you doing? (*There is no answer.*) What's wrong with the locker? . . . (*Hesketh goes on taking things out.*) Have they given you the push on the spot? . . . Anyway I'd no idea you were smoking . . . I should have covered up for you if I'd known . . . I'm not that mean.

WATSON (*to Hesketh*) Come on, lad.
Hesketh takes his stuff and goes to another locker and starts putting it in.

GREGG What are you doing that for?

WATSON Off you go.

GREGG Oh, I see . . . you're frightened of foot and mouth disease ... And I can use the spare locker space as well so don't worry about me.

The sending to Coventry is clearly having the reverse effect from the one intended. Gregg whistles. The men look at each other. Watson is furious. Gregg wins on points.

NARRATOR Hesketh hadn't long to wait. Soon he was summoned to Mr Collett's office, but of course Mr Collett never mentioned smoking in the stores. Hesketh didn't know what to think.

Mr Collett's office

COLLETT So you see, Hesketh, it's a case of expelling the drones. Do you understand?

HESKETH Yes, sir.

COLLETT From top to bottom. So tell them, will you? Tell any drones you know of. Do you know some? Yes I daresay you do but it wouldn't be proper to tell. False loyalty, Hesketh, is the mark of the feeble minded boy. And that's all you are—a—boy. How old are you?

HESKETH Sixteen.

COLLETT Sixteen. It's pathetic. But at least you're at the start. Up the wrong path a little way but not too far. Still time to turn back and make it up. *Elsewhere*. I'm sorry, Hesketh, but you must have expected it.

HESKETH Yes, sir, I expected it.

COLLETT Well then, you must have been prepared. It can't have been all that much of a surprise.

HESKETH I came prepared, sir, but you never gave me a chance to explain.

COLLETT I'm afraid you can't explain. It's not a matter of opinion. It's a matter of fact. And your future.

HESKETH But, sir, the report wouldn't sound so bad without the other things and I've not been given a chance to say anything about them. When the stores foreman caught me smoking, he was off like lightning. He didn't look twice. I was putting it out. I really was. Two more drags and it would have been over. It was no more than a tab end. I've known some blokes make a habit of popping in there for a smoke. And nobody caught them and the stores are still standing up.

COLLETT Just a moment, Hesketh. One thing at a time. I was talking about you and the technical college. Now you've brought up quite a new thing.

HESKETH Yes, sir, but . . . they must all add up. Uncle Harry, er . . . Mr Watson told me after that bad report last term that I'd never get the sack just for being bad at long division. He made a joke of it.

COLLETT Now just remind me. When were you reported for smoking, Hesketh.

HESKETH You remember, sir. Smoking in the H.S.F. stores. Mr Glassford rang you up about it.

COLLETT *(looking in his desk diary)* And that would be?

HESKETH Last Tuesday.

COLLETT Last Tuesday. And you thought that would seal your fate?

HESKETH Well, if it wasn't that what else could it have been? It's the first time I've been caught doing anything.

COLLETT And if Mr Glassford reported you I'm certain he was quite right.

HESKETH He said he had to because of a rule being a rule.

COLLETT Yes, Hesketh, I'm sure he did. But he's not here at the moment. Just us two. So don't bother with his side of the story. Just tell me yours.

Locker room area

FIRST MAN They'll move him to another section perhaps. They won't get rid of him—they'll always give him another chance somewhere else.

WATSON Not for that, they won't. He's out.

THIRD MAN That's life.

SECOND

MAN What if they'd caught him slipping through the gates to get your cigarettes?

WATSON You what?

110

SECOND
MAN   What if they'd caught him slipping through the gates to get your cigarettes? Or clocking on for you. Wouldn't he have got the same then?

WATSON No he wouldn't. I'd have taken the blame.
There's silence as they think this over.
Hesketh comes in, walks over to his locker and takes out his scarf and his jacket. They watch him.

WATSON Did you get them, Brian lad? It makes me see red. Well then . . . don't you worry . . . there's better jobs. (*Hesketh nods.*) They're paying you up to the end of the week though, aren't they? They aren't cheese-paring to that extent. (*Hesketh nods again.*) Have a cup of tea, lad. There's plenty.
Hesketh drinks the tea and looks a bit tearful.
Gregg looks on sideways, though he goes on with his work.

WATSON You should have told him that lots worse things go on than smoking in the H.S.F. stores.

HESKETH (*after a pause*) I did.

WATSON (*looking a bit worried*) I suppose if you're caught red-handed you've got to expect to get it for smoking, though. (*Hesketh just looks at him.*) It's a big game, all this bosses and men. You've got to watch their every move.

HESKETH He didn't say anything to me about smoking. *I* told *him.*

WATSON Didn't talk about the H.S.F. stores?

HESKETH No. It didn't seem to matter.

WATSON How do you mean, it didn't seem to matter? Of course it matters. That's why you got the sack.

HESKETH I got the sack for other things.

WATSON Worse things than smoking in them stores?

HESKETH Must be. Worse things to him. Reports and things.

WATSON Reports about what.

HESKETH School reports.

WATSON School reports. You must be joking. This firm has never cared a damn about how folk do at school. It doesn't come into it. Nobody ever got the push for messing up his long division.

HESKETH (*shrugs*) That's what he said.

111

FIRST MAN That's what he said.

WATSON But that's not what he meant. Believe me. (*Very deliberately*) The reports he's been getting weren't written by anybody at the Tech. and they're nothing to do with geometry and machine drawing. They're reports from inside and they're going straight to him. It's all a cover up what he's told you. I reckon he heard about you from somebody else.

FIRST MAN Who else could he hear from? Mr Glassford would never tell him.

WATSON Who's talking about Glassford?

SECOND
MAN If you think it's Gregg you'll have to prove it.

WATSON Come on then.

They stop and look at Gregg who is carrying on working. Watson drifts up to Gregg and speaks beside him.

WATSON You've been in the boss's pocket since the day you came. You're the sort he likes. I can tell as soon as look at you. (*He gives Gregg a vicious push.*)

SECOND
MAN You won't prove a thing with itchy fists.

THIRD MAN He's right, Sam.

There is general approval from the men.

WATSON What chance did he give young Hesketh? There wasn't much charity about that.

SECOND
MAN Young Hesketh was caught smoking.

WATSON Aye. And *this* one was caught. By me. Why would a lad stay behind after work and have to get the key for his locker? Because he was with the boss.
What would anybody be telling the boss all that length of time?

SECOND
MAN Would you like us to tell you?

WATSON No I wouldn't. Because I know. And he's going to *pay* for it.

Watson makes a dash at Gregg. Seeing that this has gone too far, the men get hold of him and disarm him.

THIRD MAN (*as they struggle*) Hop it, lad.

GREGG   I can look after myself. (*Going up to Watson who by this time is in a heap.*) Watson, I'm sorry you broke your silence. You were better quiet. You made more sense. I don't need to tell anybody about you. You tell them yourself without meaning to. I'm sorry Hesketh got the sack. They got the wrong man this time. But they won't always miss.

WATSON   What about that? That's as good as a threat. Did you hear him? You're my witnesses. All of you.

GREGG   I wouldn't depend on them if I were you.
         The buzzer is heard.

Collett's office

COLLETT So the lad played straight into my hands, told me all about the smoking affair and the report Glassford was supposed to make. You didn't have any report on Hesketh, did you, Thomas?

THOMAS   No, sir. I didn't.

COLLETT And if Mr Glassford had made it you would have seen it automatically?

THOMAS   Of course, sir.

COLLETT Well. All I can say is that communications at Collett & Son need an overhaul. Yes, Thomas?

THOMAS   Yes, sir.

COLLETT (*on intercom*) Miss Carey.

THOMAS   So, sir, may I ask where do we go from here?

COLLETT Well, Glassford can't deny he failed to make a report. And he knows it's a serious offence. Doesn't he?

THOMAS   Yes, sir.

COLLETT 9.0 a.m. tomorrow Glassford reports to me (*pause—Thomas reacts*) . . . transfer to the packing section.

THOMAS   Yes, sir. They are milder in packing, truly.

COLLETT And Clarke goes from H.S.F. stores to the pressing shop. See how Watson likes that.

THOMAS   He won't, sir.

COLLETT How long do you think he'll last—three weeks?

THOMAS   Perhaps two.

COLLETT Even better. (*Enter Miss Carey*) Ah, tea.
         The play ends with a close up of Thomas looking old.

Time Hurries On

by Fay Weldon

The Cast

Christine, *aged sixteen*
Ellen, *her mother*
Barbara, *aged sixteen*
Tony, *her boy friend*
Mrs Patterson, *aged seventy-two*

Christine doesn't really know how to feel towards Barbara.
Christine's own home and her warm sensible mother seem
rather dull compared with Barbara's plans for a romantic
life. At any rate, although only sixteen, Barbara is planning to run away and get married—what's more she needs
Christine's help. Barbara, of course, is quite certain that
older generations didn't have either these problems or
these excitements. A seventy-two-year-old woman whom
Christine sometimes helps looks at things differently!

Time Hurries On

As the introductory captions come on the screen, we see a boy and a girl walking and then embracing. At the same time we hear a popular song being sung off screen.

Leaves that are Green

"I was 21 years when I wrote this song;
I'm 22 now but I won't be for long.
Time hurries on
and the leaves that are green turn to brown
and they wither with the wind
and they crumble in your hand.
Once my heart was filled with the love of a girl:
I held her close
but she faded in the night
Like a poem I meant to write
and the leaves that are green turn to brown."

Cut to:

Christine's house

Christine is practising her guitar, and singing.

CHRISTINE And they wither with the wind
And they wither with the wind
There is a knock on the window. We see Barbara, outside the window with Tony. Christine goes to the door, and opens it. All three are now at the door. Tony goes. The door is closed. Christine and Barbara are in the hall.
CHRISTINE That was Tony.
BARBARA I should hope so.
CHRISTINE But you're not supposed to see him.
BARBARA Oh you're so dull.

CHRISTINE What do you want? I'm trying to practise.

BARBARA You're so selfish. All you ever think about is yourself. You're the most selfish person I've ever met. Is that clock right?

CHRISTINE Yes, why? I thought Tony had gone back to Scotland.

BARBARA Don't you think he's absolutely smashing?

CHRISTINE I've told you. I don't know what you see in him.

BARBARA How can I explain. Perhaps it's what he sees in me. All the other boys just care about what you look like—he cares about what I feel like—what I am.

CHRISTINE That's what he says.

BARBARA I'm sure I'm never going to meet anyone like him again, ever. The boys round here are so awful. They're so dull. They get dull jobs and they lead dull lives and they're dreary.

CHRISTINE They do pay the rent.

BARBARA You're dreary too. Sometimes you sound like everyone's mother.

CHRISTINE I'm only trying to talk sense.

BARBARA I'm tired of sense. It's been going on for so long. Going to school and wearing uniform and going to bed at the right time and getting up at the right time and telling your parents where you are. It's time for big decisions and I'll want your help.

CHRISTINE My help? What do you want me to do, Barbara?

BARBARA You to say I'm with you when I'm not.

CHRISTINE I knew it. Oh Barbara.

BARBARA (mimicking) Oh Barbara! All anyone ever says to me is oh Barbara! I'm not such a monster. Just because I want to live my own life in my own way. Why does everyone round here have to be so stupid? They sound much nicer in Scotland. Tony says Glasgow's a real swinging city, much better than London. Don't you think I look prettier since Tony fell in love with me?

CHRISTINE Yes.

BARBARA Then it must be all right, mustn't it?

CHRISTINE What must? It might just be getting older. I've been looking rather better myself lately. My spots are going.

BARBARA	I hadn't noticed.
CHRISTINE	I have a terrible feeling you're about to do something stupid.
BARBARA	No, I'm not.
CHRISTINE	You're only sixteen. It's not old enough to make big decisions.
BARBARA	Romeo and Juliet got married at fourteen. No one laughed at them.
CHRISTINE	You're not Juliet.
BARBARA	No, thank heaven. The soppy fool. (*She looks at the clock.*) Ten to four. This operation is timed to the minute.
CHRISTINE	Operation, what operation?
BARBARA	Oh doesn't time go slowly sometimes. Where's your mother?
CHRISTINE	Upstairs, ironing.
BARBARA	Upstairs? Why does she do her ironing upstairs? How they spend their lives. Isn't it tragic. Tony is going to wear nothing but drip dry. I hate ironing.
CHRISTINE	Suppose he doesn't want to? I mean he is real. He's not a dream.
BARBARA	Of course he'll want to. You don't understand love, that's your trouble.
CHRISTINE	Perhaps I don't. I'm sure my father loves my mother, but he still makes a terrible fuss about his shirts. I suppose that's how love ends up. Sort of every-day.
BARBARA	Not ours. You don't know Tony.
	Tony's face appears against the window—pointing in the direction of the front door. Barbara rushes to open it. Christine tags along behind. A suitcase stands on the step. There is no sign of Tony.
CHRISTINE	It's a suitcase.
BARBARA	No, dear; it's an elephant.
CHRISTINE	What's it doing there?
BARBARA	It's come back for its handkerchief. Elephants never forget.
CHRISTINE	Barbara, please, whose is it?
BARBARA	It belongs to the circus I expect. Whose do you think?
CHRISTINE	(*furious*) I'm going to get my mother, this minute.
BARBARA	It's my suitcase, idiot.

CHRISTINE Why did Tony have it?

BARBARA Well, I can hardly walk round the streets with it. Everyone would guess and then someone would tell my mum. No one in this town ever minds their own business.

CHRISTINE Guess what?

BARBARA We're eloping. We're going to Scotland. You can get married there at sixteen.

CHRISTINE They'll kill you.

BARBARA They won't find me to kill me. Not till I'm a married woman.

CHRISTINE Are you going to live in Scotland?

BARBARA I expect so. Tony's got a lovely little flat in Sauchiehall Street in the very middle of Glasgow. Some of the year we'll live there. We may come south in the winter, who can say?

CHRISTINE Can I come and stay with you in the holidays? It does get rather boring here, you are quite right.

BARBARA Of course, everyone can come.

CHRISTINE Barbara (*Barbara looks up.*) I thought Sauchiehall Street was all shops. You know, one of those big shopping streets.

BARBARA What of it? The flat's above a shop, I expect.

CHRISTINE He's not having you on, is he?

BARBARA Don't be so silly; he wouldn't lie to me.

CHRISTINE Because you don't know his family or friends or anything, and sometimes it's hard to tell.

BARBARA What kind of horrible, suspicious, mean minded person are you? I *love* Tony. I know.

CHRISTINE Oh, I've never loved anyone. I don't know what it feels like. I love my mother and my father, of course, but I suppose that's different.

There is another tap at the window. It is Tony again. Barbara opens the window this time.

TONY Hey, Ba.

BARBARA Darling! Has something gone wrong? Have they found out?

TONY No, no, no. Nothing ever goes wrong for me.

BARBARA What then?

TONY Have you got £5?

BARBARA £5? Well . . . just about. But it's all my savings. What do you want it for?

TONY We're going to travel first class on the train. In style.

BARBARA First class, but surely . . .

TONY We ought to start as we're going to go on. Nothing but the best. You deserve it, don't you? Look after yourself, darling. Don't be late. I love you. (*And he takes the money and is gone.*)

CHRISTINE What did he want?

BARBARA Nothing. Why hasn't my mother rung yours yet to check on me? You can't rely on them for anything, can you? Not even spying.

CHRISTINE My mother doesn't spy on me.

BARBARA You never do anything worth spying on, that's all that is. They're all alike. If my mother loved me she wouldn't keep nagging me and trying to stop me seeing Tony. We're going to the pictures together, you and me, in ten minutes.

CHRISTINE Are we?

BARBARA Yes. You can carry the suitcase down. If you're carrying it no one will think anything.

CHRISTINE What are we going to see?

BARBARA I don't know. It's nothing to do with me. You're the one who's going to see it. Me, I'm going to slip out the fire exit and round the corner to the station. When they meet us coming out there'll be just you, not both of us, because Tony and me will be off to Scotland, and then they'll be sorry.

CHRISTINE What for?

BARBARA Driving me to do this. Forbidding me to see him after ten o'clock at night as if I was a child. Laughing at the way I feel as if I didn't count. I'm old enough to be married. I will be married, I'll show them. I'm going to be so happy, Christine. For ever and ever and ever.

CHRISTINE They'll kill me.

BARBARA I've got to get on the train with no one knowing.

CHRISTINE We'd better hide the suitcase then. If my mother sees it she'll guess. I'll put it behind the side gate.

BARBARA   Your mother is quite bright, isn't she? She's alright really, for a parent.

CHRISTINE   I think I ought to tell her, Barbara. It's not like breaking a window, or cheating in exams. It's getting married. It's your whole life.

BARBARA   You're my friend, aren't you?

CHRISTINE   Yes.

BARBARA   Then help me. (*She suddenly hears some noise from above.*) Quick, hide the suitcase.

But it's too late. Christine's mother, Ellen, is coming down the stairs and has seen it. Ellen is a shrewd pleasant woman. She carries a pile of ironing.

ELLEN   (*half joking*) Mind you marry a millionaire, Christine, or at any rate someone who doesn't insist on a clean shirt every morning. Hello, Barbara. Does your mother know you're out?

BARBARA   Yes, actually, ring her if you like. Though she'll be ringing you in a minute to check up. You wait.

ELLEN   It's all right, dear. I believe you, thousands wouldn't. How's Tony?

BARBARA   He's very well. No one ever says "How's Tony?" at home, not like that. If they say "How's Tony?", it's only because they hope he's dropped dead.

ELLEN   It's very worrying having daughters. Some daughters.

BARBARA   It's very worrying having parents. Some parents.

ELLEN   (*who has meanwhile been observing Christine's efforts to stand in front of the suitcase*) Whose suitcase?

BARBARA   That's Christine's.

ELLEN   (*surprised*) Christine's? That!

CHRISTINE   Well not exactly mine.

ELLEN   What do you mean?

CHRISTINE   (*wildly*) It belongs to Mrs Patterson. You know the old lady above the fish shop. The one I visit.

ELLEN   Why have you got her suitcase?

CHRISTINE   It's full of her things.

ELLEN   Why?

CHRISTINE   They had to be washed and ironed.

ELLEN   Here? I didn't see you.

BARBARA	No, at my place. I did them.
ELLEN	*You* did?
BARBARA	Christine isn't the only one who's good to old ladies.
ELLEN	(*advancing on the suitcase*) This had to be seen to be believed.
BARBARA	Don't open it now. We're just off.
ELLEN	Just off where?
CHRISTINE	To visit Mrs Patterson. To take her back the suitcase.
ELLEN	But you're supposed to be practising, Christine.
CHRISTINE	Oh, I shall sing to Mrs Patterson.
ELLEN	Sing to her? Does she like that?
BARBARA	Well, she has to, doesn't she? She's helpless.
CHRISTINE	Barbara!
ELLEN	(*advancing again*) Let me see—that suit . . .
	But the telephone goes just in time and she is obliged to answer it.
BARBARA	Saved! Unless Mrs Patterson wears baby-doll nighties in black nylon.
ELLEN	(*on the phone*) Angela! Yes I've got Barbara here. No not Tony . . . Is he indeed! In that case I certainly won't let them out of my sight, either of them. Don't worry. No, it will be all right. Cheerio Angela. Cheerio.
	She puts the receiver down. She smiles, benignly. They don't trust her and they're right not to.
ELLEN	(*blandly*) Going to see Mrs Patterson, are you? What kind girls. I'll come down the road with you.
BARBARA	(*dismayed*) You'll what?
ELLEN	I'm going to the laundrette. I can see Mrs Patterson's front door from there. You can play the guitar to her, Christine. And you can unpack the suitcase, Barbara and we'll wave to each other out of the window. And then we'll all come home together.
	As they make their way out, we hear that song again.

I threw a pebble in a brook
And watched the ripples run away
And they never made a sound
And the leaves that are green turn to brown
And they wither

The outside of a laundrette is seen, and the song fades to street noises.

Mrs Patterson's room

BARBARA (*looking out of the window*) Look! She's sitting right next to the window. The cunning old bag.

CHRISTINE (*looking too*) Don't talk about my mother like that.

BARBARA Wave at her, or she'll think something's wrong.

CHRISTINE (*sarcastic: waving*) You think she doesn't know already?

BARBARA Now what am I going to do? Tony'll go mad if I miss that train.

CHRISTINE When the red light goes on she'll have to put the soap and the bleach in. Then you'll have thirty seconds to get out through the front door.

BARBARA Then we'll have to watch for the red light.

MRS P. Now, what can I do for you this time?

CHRISTINE (*surprised*) What do you mean?

MRS P. How can I help you? Isn't that what you want?

CHRISTINE It's . . . it's me that's supposed to help you.

MRS P. Why?

CHRISTINE Because . . . because . . . we're young and . . . and . . . you're old.

MRS P. Your legs work better than mine do, I'll say that for you. I'm not sure about your brains.

BARBARA But I don't think you'd understand.

MRS P. I might.

BARBARA People over twenty are completely different from people under twenty. And you're eighty.

MRS P. Seventy-two. I'm just a chicken. I have a very good friend of ninety-two. Someone proposed to her the other day. She didn't accept either. She said he just wanted someone to do his washing.

BARBARA But honestly Mrs Patterson I don't mean to be rude but by the time you're seventy-two you must be set in your ways.

MRS P. Times change; people don't, my girl. What do you mean set in my ways? I only wish I was. Quite enough happens in my life let me tell you, without me looking for more.

BARBARA	How can it?
MRS P.	They're moving me without so much as a by-your-leave. I've lived here for twenty years. I like it. It's my place. They say I can't manage the stairs. What rubbish.
CHRISTINE	Where are you going?
MRS P.	To some poky little council flat for old people, with an alarm bell outside the door, and community dinners. I know what they'll be like. Mush. Just because you're old they think you haven't got teeth. People are very kind and well meaning, but they don't understand.
BARBARA	I know exactly what you mean.
MRS P.	The only thing is they're usually right. Don't forget that. My teeth aren't all that good if I'm going to be honest.
CHRISTINE	Well it's obvious, Mrs Patterson, that you can't manage the stairs any more. It's only sensible to move.
MRS P.	I have trouble doing the sensible thing, dear. You're lucky if you don't. I've manage very well so far, with a little help from nice people like you. But I suppose people will get bored with helping sooner or later, so I've got to be sensible, like it or not. I might even quite enjoy it when I'm there. I'm not saying I will, but I might.
	Barbara isn't listening any more, she's over at the window with Christine whispering.
CHRISTINE	The minute the red light goes on, I'll shriek and you rush out. Keep talking to her or she'll guess.
MRS P.	Is there something interesting at the window?
BARBARA	No, no. It's just nice sitting here that's all.
CHRISTINE	Couldn't you get tomorrow's train? If he loves you he'll wait for you.
BARBARA	No, he won't. You know what boys are like. Especially Tony. He can't help it. It's just that girls chase him all the time.
CHRISTINE	Oh, it doesn't sound like true love to me.
BARBARA	*(furious)* What do you know about anything?
MRS P.	Perhaps it's my ears, but I don't seem able to hear what you're saying.
BARBARA	I was just saying how awful it is the way other people try to stop you doing what you want to all the time.

MRS P. No one ever stopped me doing anything. I wish they had, sometimes. Will you have some tea, Christine?

CHRISTINE (*dying for a cup but unable to leave her post*) No, thank you. I'm not thirsty.

MRS P. I've got some lovely chocolate cake. I made it myself. You'd like some of that, wouldn't you?

CHRISTINE (*who would*) I'm slimming.

MRS P. (*to Barbara*) You'd like some?

BARBARA Yes, thanks. (*Christine is furious.*)

MRS P. What did you say your name was?

BARBARA Barbara.

MRS P. You remind me of someone but I can't see your face clearly.

BARBARA I'm sorry, are your eyes bad?

MRS P. It's not my eyes, it's your face.

BARBARA (*taken aback*) Oh!

MRS P. It will get better in time, I expect. Don't worry.

BARBARA What's wrong with it?

MRS P. It's not all of a piece yet. Young people's faces are like that. A bit of mother and a bit of father, a bit of all the other faces you've ever known. You get your own face in time.

BARBARA (*to Christine*) What's she talking about? (*to Mrs P*) And I'm certainly not in the least like my mother.

MRS P. Probably more than you think.

BARBARA Oh no, all she can think about is polishing furniture. I have principles and ideals.

CHRISTINE Is that what they are. I'd never have guessed.

BARBARA I'm true to my feelings.

MRS P. You do what you want when you want, you mean.

BARBARA No, I don't; I mean love—doing what your heart says, not your brain. You feel silly saying it, but it's true.

MRS P. How old did you say you were?

BARBARA I didn't, but I'm sixteen, nearly seventeen.

MRS P. When I was sixteen it was 1914. I was married when I was sixteen.

BARBARA Were you? Were you honestly? Well then it's not too young is it? Not really.

126

MRS P.   Too young. I didn't think about it like that. I didn't really think about it at all. It just seemed the only thing I could do.

BARBARA   Why was that?

MRS P.   I was in service. A skivvy. I got up at six, finished at eleven—

BARBARA   In the morning?

MRS P.   No. At night. I had six days off a year, and got paid six pounds.

BARBARA   Six pounds a week.

MRS P.   No, six pounds a year, dear. Slaving for other people because that's what it was. Slavery.

BARBARA   Why did you do it?

MRS P.   Because I had to live. It wasn't like now, picking and choosing.

BARBARA   How awful.

MRS P.   Was it? I suppose so. I had somewhere to live and enough to eat, and my legs worked. Perhaps I should have been grateful. But I was never the grateful type. They said he wasn't right for me but I took no notice of them.

BARBARA   But he was, wasn't he?

MRS P.   He promised me the earth. I believed him. Money and fun and comfort and love. It's not true that all you need is love the way the song says. You need a roof over your head and food in the cupboard.

BARBARA   But he gave you that as well, didn't he?

MRS P.   He did not. Come the war six months after we were married and off he went. A volunteer the very first day—he needn't have done. He was no more suited to marriage than jam is to kippers.

BARBARA   But you loved him?

MRS P.   I was expecting my baby by then. It was never really love in the first place, I expect, just wanting to get away. And three years without him, living in a tiny room with no heating and not enough to eat, with a little baby—it has to be a very grand kind of love to get the better of that. It wasn't.

BARBARA   I'm sorry.

MRS P.   So was I, believe you me. He came back from the war
         an invalid. I nursed him for twenty years, until he got
         pneumonia and died.

BARBARA Twenty years!

MRS P.   It's for better or worse, my girl. Remember that when you
         get married. With any luck it might be for better, but it
         might well not be.

BARBARA (*unsurely*) I'd nurse Tony for twenty years, I would.

MRS P.   When he died I was only thirty-nine. Quite a young
         woman.

BARBARA Young!

MRS P.   Not even a chicken, dear, just a chick. Life goes on a long,
         long time; don't be in too much of a hurry to start it.

BARBARA That's what my mother keeps saying. Well, I can do with-
         out her, thank you very much.

MRS P.   Can you? Well, you'll need her when the babies come.

BARBARA I can manage on my own.

MRS P.   We can all manage if we have to.

CHRISTINE Your mother's not as bad as you think. If she didn't love
         you she wouldn't care what you did one way or the other.

BARBARA Be quiet and watch that light. (*There is a pause while we see
         the two girls' faces.*) Surely it should have come on by
         now. If he goes without me I shall die.
         *Mrs Patterson has been over at her bureau, taking out a photo-
         graph album. She beckons Barbara over.*

MRS P.   Barbara. Come over here. That's a picture of me just be-
         fore I was married. And that's Eddie, my husband. Poor
         Eddie, it wasn't fair to him. I should have had enough
         sense for both of us. He believed the things he said, you
         know. All those promises. It was just he didn't know how
         to bring them about. I know who you remind me of now.

BARBARA Who?

MRS P.   (*pointing to her own photograph*) Me. Poor little girl. So long
         ago it hardly seems like me.

BARBARA I don't think that seems like me at all, and you didn't
         really love him; you only thought you did.

MRS P.   Love? What do you know about love? Love is washing up
         day after day, cooking for the children, cleaning the home.

128

BARBARA   Times have changed. You can get divorced if it doesn't work out.

MRS P.   Oh, can you? Perhaps you'll have children. A woman with children can't just think of herself; she has to think of them. No, marriage is for good and all.

CHRISTINE   Look, the red light. Oh, Barbara, don't go.
But it's too late for Christine to change her mind now. Barbara seizes her suitcase and leaves without so much as a goodbye.

MRS P.   Where was she off to in such a hurry?

CHRISTINE   I should have stopped her.

MRS P.   Her? She's a big girl now. Too big to stop. She'll have to stop herself. Perhaps she'll learn, perhaps she won't. Now we can have that cup of tea?
Cut to shot of a train rushing past, and then:
Cut to:

The inside of the compartment

Tony and Barbara together in a first class carriage. They snuggle happily.

BARBARA   Darling. First class. Isn't it lovely? I've never travelled first class in all my life.

TONY   You always will from now on.

BARBARA   It makes my heart turn over when you say things like that. But £5 extra. We could rent eight weeks of telly for that.

TONY   Don't say things like that.

BARBARA   What's the matter.

TONY   You sounded just like your mother.

BARBARA   I'm sorry. Did I really?

TONY   Yes, you did. You won't turn into a worrier, will you?

BARBARA   Never.

TONY   There's no need to. You can trust me Barbara. I made £6 on the horses today. I've got a system. £6.

BARBARA   (*astonished*) You what?

TONY   I only used the money you gave so just in case it didn't come in we'd still have enough for the tickets. I'm not a fool. I'm not rash and it did come in. I knew it would. Everything's going right today. We're saved.

BARBARA (*faintly*) Saved?

TONY I was a bit behind with the rent for the flat. Not much, just a bit.

BARBARA It *is* where you said it was, isn't it, Tony? In the centre?

TONY Well, more or less.

BARBARA How much less?

TONY I told you, don't be a worrier. I'll look after you.

BARBARA But that £5. That was my money. It was forty hours baby sitting.

TONY What's yours is mine as well as vice versa. That's marriage. You don't grudge it to me, Barbara?

BARBARA No, only . . .

TONY Only what?

BARBARA What Mrs Patterson said. He meant all the promises, he just didn't have the strength to carry them out.

TONY What are you talking about? Who did?

BARBARA Just someone a long time ago.

TONY Isn't it nice in here. We can get to know each other. There's been so little time really, everyone trying to stop us being together. There must be lots of things about you I still don't know. And you about me, I suppose.

BARBARA Yes, does this train stop before Glasgow?

TONY Yes, Crewe, Carlisle. Why?

BARBARA Oh, nothing.

Barbara doesn't reply but it's fairly clear the sooner she can get off the better.

We see them again for the last time from the corridor, as the song returns, and the final captions come onto the screen.

Last Bus

By Keith Dewhurst

The Cast

Bus conductor (*Irish*)
Bus driver (*West Indian*)
Peter
Carol, *his fiancée*
Four boys, all about seventeen: Robbo, *the leader*
                                             Dave
                                             Arthur
                                             Colin
Mr Phillips, *an elderly man*
Mrs Smith
An interviewer

In a large town in the south of England the last bus of the day sets off with a few passengers on board. The conductor is Irish, the driver is West Indian. Four youths, aged about seventeen, board the bus in obviously high spirits. They make fun of the conductor when he comes to collect their fares, and the eldest boy, the leader of the group, refuses to pay. The conductor stops the bus and threatens that the bus will not move again until the boys get off. He goes and talks to the driver. There are now four other passengers left on board: an old man, a middle-class woman, a young man and his fiancée. The bus waits in a lonely road near a housing estate and the boys eventually run off, but they return as the conductor mounts the platform. They beat him up, then knock him to the ground and begin to kick him. They then run off. Neither the passengers nor the driver comes to the aid of the conductor.

The second half of the programme is set in the studio some time after the incident. Each of the passengers, the crew and one of the boys are interviewed and cross-examined to try to find out why they behaved as they did on that particular night.

Last Bus

It is night. There are not many people about in the streets—only the occasional figure hurrying on his way. By a parade of small shops, the kind that cluster near the edge of a town, four seventeen-year-old boys are larking about in the patchy street lighting.

Looking along the street the camera shows a double-decker bus in the distance. It draws near and one of the youths does a little dance by the kerb to make it stop. The others jeer and jostle round the bus stop. As the bus pulls up, the youths leap on, clatter up the stairs, and pile into a couple of seats.

Their noisy pushing and giggling attracts the disapproving looks of the other passengers.

The conductor is on the lower deck, and about to collect fares from Peter and Carol.

CONDUC. Where to, mate?

PETER Two to the depot, please.

CONDUC. Two one and fours, please. Two and eight, please. Thank you. (*The conductor moves up to an oldish man.*) Where to, Pop?

MR P. All the way, mate.

CONDUC.	One and four, please.
MR P.	Ta.
COND.	Thank you. (*The camera goes back to Carol and Peter as the conductor goes upstairs.*)
PETER	Give us a kiss.
CAROL	No.
PETER	Who's looking?
CAROL	Everybody.
PETER	We're getting married next week.
CAROL	Well, what you waiting for?
PETER	He's watching us.
CAROL	Who?
PETER	The conductor.
	They kiss.
CAROL	You are awful, Peter! You'll do anything like that, won't you? That's why I love you. You know that, don't you?
PETER	Yes.
CONDUC.	(*Coming along the top deck to the boys.*) Right, lads.
ROBBO	Three halves.
CONDUC.	There's four of you.
ROBBO	Four halves.
CONDUC.	How old are you?
DAVE	An 'undred.
CONDUC.	You can't be half fare then, can you?

ARTHUR (*sarcastically*) Clever!

ROBBO No, he's right. Eight halves.

ARTHUR Eh?

ROBBO Four wholes.

ARTHUR Genius! Genius!

CONDUC. (*fairly patiently*) Come on, lads. Where are you bound for?

COLIN All the way.

CONDUC. Right, that will be eightpence each, please. (*Some coins are handed over, and he counts them.*) There's only two bob here.

DAVE He can count.

CONDUC. Yes, four eights—two and eight.

ROBBO Yes, that's right.

CONDUC. That's right. So I want another eightpence and no cheek.

ROBBO I've given it to you.

ARTHUR What do you mean, cheek?

DAVE (*in a put-on voice*) Darling, give me your cheek.

ARTHUR No, he needs a shave.

CONDUC. Come on, another eightpence, please.

ROBBO I've given it.

CONDUC. Are you saying you are all paid for?

ROBBO Yes. (*pointing to Colin*) He's not with this lot.

CONDUC. (*his patience fast going.*) Now look, son, do yourself a favour. This is your last chance.

ROBBO He's paid.

CONDUC. Has he? Where's his ticket then?

COLIN Must have dropped it.

CONDUC. Well, where did you drop it?

COLIN How do I know?

CONDUCT. Look, are you paying?

ROBBO (*with surprise and pretend anger*) Twice?

CONDUCT. (*strongly*) Now, the one that hasn't paid get off. (*There is a pause.*) Do you hear me talking to you? Now, this bus isn't going to move until the one that hasn't paid gets off.

ROBBO It's that woman up there. She's the one. She ain't paid.

ARTHUR What do you mean, that one?

ROBBO Yes, with the moustache.

DAVE (*shouting*) Oi, Mrs!

CONDUC. Oh, shut up, mate!

DAVE Oh, she won't talk to me.

MRS SMITH (*at last looking round*) You ought to be ashamed of yourselves.

ROBBO Oh, shut up!

CONDUCT. Now, look here, son . . . (*He goes to touch Robbo*)

ROBBO (*violently*) Don't you put your filthy Irish hands on me!

CONDUCT. I never touched you.

ROBBO Your hands are filthy.

ARTHUR It's fingering the money.

ROBBO I don't care what it is. He's a filthy Irish git.

DAVE He's got a face like a potato.

ARTHUR Yeah, that's with eating them, isn't it? Look, they're growing out of 'is ears.

CONDUC. Shut up, the lot of you!

MRS SMITH I'm going for a policeman.

ROBBO You're what!

CONDUCT. No, no, sit down, lady. (*He rings the bell for the bus to stop.*) I'll have a word with the driver. Stay where you are.
(*We see him go quickly down the stairs. The few passengers on the lower deck look up. The bus has stopped in an apparently deserted place. We see a close-up of Carol as she looks round.*)

CAROL What's happening?

PETER   He's got off.
MR P.   (*explaining*) Trouble upstairs.
PETER   Eh?
MR P.   Trouble.
        *Cut to the front of the bus, where the conductor is standing in
        the road talking up to the driver in the cab.*
DRIVER What's the story, mate?
CONDUC. Oh, it's the same as bloody usual. Well, you might have
        come round.
DRIVER Will they get off quiet?

CONDUC. I hope so.
     (*But he doesn't look very hopeful. We go back to the top deck again.
     The boys are well settled into their seats.*)
ROBBO You know what the driver is, don't you?
ARTHUR What?
ROBBO A spade.
DAVE Are you sure of that?
ROBBO I saw him, didn't I?
ARTHUR How far are we from home?
COLIN Not far.

ROBBO   Oh, another free ride then.

DAVE   Yes.

ARTHUR   So who's for off then?

ROBBO   Bloody stuffed gits, bloody bastards.

MRS SMITH   You're a disgrace to the name of Britain.

But they have hardly heard Arthur waves a hand at her, as they all clatter down the stairs, finally tumbling off the platform. They run down the road a little way.

The conductor has looked round, and he and the driver watch them go.

DRIVER Eh, it looks like you've done it.

CONDUC. I thought so. You know, I thought as soon as we got to the housing estate that was the time to press the bell.

DRIVER Come on . . . let's get out of here. (*He turns back to the driving seat.*)

CONDUC. Right.

The conductor walks back, along the side of the bus. Unexpectedly we see the four youths again : they have not moved far away. Robbo is pointing. The group start moving; just as the conductor mounts the platform, two of the boys pull him back, and a third swings him

round so that his back is against the side of the bus.
Cut to inside the bus, where the few passengers have become sud-
denly aware that something is happening. Peter and Carol stand
up, and Carol begins to move.

PETER   (*calming her, and holding her back*) It's all right, Carol! It's all
right!
Cut back to the outside of the bus again. Robbo is about to punch
the conductor in the stomach. As he does so, we see the woman,
Mrs Smith, stand up inside the bus and come down the stairs.

MRS SMITH   Help him somebody, help him.

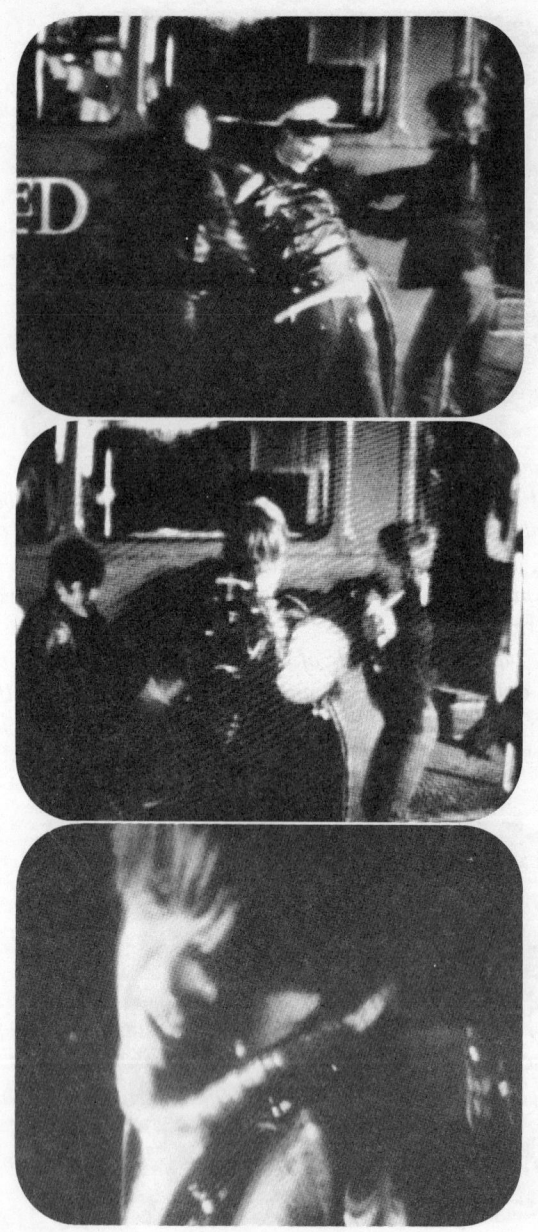

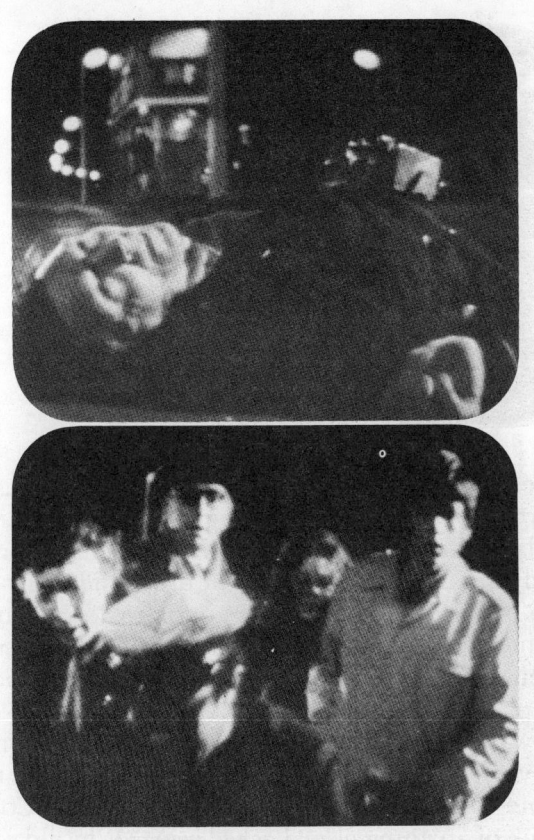

MR P. You help him woman, I'm seventy-five.
Outside again, we see the pain on the conductor's face, and then Robbo knocks his head against the side of the bus. A series of shots show us the driver in his cabin, Peter and Carol in the bus, and the boys kicking the conductor on the ground.
Only when the boys run off, do the passengers start to help, and then the incident ends.
We now cut to a television studio, and see an interviewer, who is speaking to the camera.

There you've been witnesses to a scene on a bus. Now, it started as an ordinary late night journey, and it finished with a punch-up: four boys onto one conductor, and nobody lifted a finger to help. The driver didn't get out of his cab. None of the passengers got off to do anything. There seemed to be no passers-by, and there didn't seem to have been anybody within miles, or at least anybody who'd help.

Now that was a scene, it was fiction and it was written by a playwright, Keith Dewhurst. Why did he want to write a scene like that? Does he just like violence? Couldn't he think of anything else? I asked him: "Why did you write a scene like that?" and he said "Because it matters to me." I can understand that. If a subject matters to somebody and that somebody happens to be a writer, then he'll write about it. But if he's a writer, why couldn't he have made the people on the bus do something? Why couldn't they get out and rescue the conductor, and then get the four boys and take them off to the police station? "At least that would have been justice, wouldn't it?" I asked him: "Why did you make the scene as grim as this?" and this is what he said: (*The interviewer picks up a note pad*.) I wrote it down. "That's not what happens," he said. "I'd like it to happen that way, but it doesn't. I don't write about what I'd like to see. I write what I see." By this time I was getting a bit hot under the collar, so I said to him "Do you think, then, that everybody who rides on buses is cowardly and selfish?" and he said "No—the people on the bus behaved as they'd got to behave." "But surely," I said, "they would have done something. Somebody would have done something. Why didn't they?" And he said "You'd better ask them!" This is exactly what we are going to do. We are going to claim the power of a law court. We're going to call all the people who were on that bus into this studio court room and we're going to ask them questions so that we can find out or try to find out why they behaved as they did on that particular night. (*The camera pulls back to show the woman*

we've seen before. She is sitting by the interviewer.) Mrs Smith, you were involved in that incident on the bus. The four boys were very rude to you, and then you saw them punch up the conductor. What's your attitude to the boys?

MRS SMITH   Well, firstly I'd like to say how ashamed I am that I didn't do more to help. You know it makes me very angry that in these days of the welfare state, when the children are offered such opportunities, that they just take them for granted and don't benefit by them.

INTERV. What opportunities are you talking about?

MRS SMITH Well there's education and free training when they leave school, and more leisure than they've ever had before, and more money. I mean, what more do they want?

INTERV. Do you suggest then that we should take these privileges away, I mean give them less money and more work?

MRS SMITH Oh, no, you couldn't do that. It would be inhuman. But if there could be some scheme, perhaps government backed that when children leave school and they don't know what to do that they could be sent for short periods to an under-developed country—to help the needy perhaps.

INTERV. It could be said, though, that you are just shipping them out of the way so that you don't have the problem. Is that right?

MRS SMITH No, no. This is nonsense. It's just to give them a sense of purpose.

INTERV. But are the boys entirely to blame, just the boys them-selves? Is it just them?

MRS SMITH No, not entirely. I think it's a question of family influence. If only the parents could give them a good example, that would be half the battle, but so often the parents take the children's side against the teachers. I mean we read about it in the papers practically every day.

INTERV. That's true, but there's a lot of evidence, isn't there, that boys like this come from very difficult homes and are dis-turbed. They need a sort of treatment; they don't just need punishment. What have you got to say to that?

MRS SMITH That's always being made an excuse. There *are* cases of course, but to my mind it's the easy way out.

INTERV. I see. You've got children yourself have you, Mrs Smith?

MRS SMITH Yes, I have: a boy and a girl.

INTERV. Tell me, what does the boy do?

MRS SMITH The boy's seventeen and he goes to a public school.

INTERV. I see. And what will he do after that?

MRS SMITH Well, actually he wants to be an artist.

INTERV. The girl?

MRS SMITH The girl's fifteen, and she's at the local grammar school. She hopes to go to a university because she wants to teach.

INTERV. Your house, the house you live in—what sort of a place is it?

MRS SMITH We have a detached house with a garden facing the common.

INTERV. So *your* children, whenever they wanted to go out and do something violent, could go out and do it in your own garden and not disturb anybody. Is that right? Compared with the other children, the lads in the bus who obviously had nothing, had no place at all in which they could do this. I don't think you're in a very good position to judge them.

MRS SMITH I think you're being unfair to me. My grandfather was a poor man; he worked very hard for everything we had.

INTERV. Thank you very much.
As the interviewer gets up to move to the next witness, we hear again a snatch of sound from the incident on the bus.

MRS SMITH Help him somebody, help him.

MR P. You help him woman; I'm seventy-five.
The interviewer has sat down next to the old man we saw on the bus, Mr Phillips.

INTERV. Mr Phillips, you witnessed a row and you saw a punch-up. What do you feel about it?

MR P. Well, I was annoyed. It was late and I wanted to get home.

INTERV. You didn't help, did you? Why not?

MR P. Well, who started it?

INTERV. Who did?

MR P. I don't know. The conductor, you know,—he was Irish.

INTERV. Does that make a difference?

MR P. Well, everybody knows the Irish. They are always getting into fights and things like that.

INTERV. So you think he might have got what he deserved?

MR P. Well, I don't know. He might have said something that annoyed the boys or made them lose their temper or something. Perhaps he hit them or touched them. I don't know. I was downstairs and they were upstairs you see.

INTERV. I see. This was obviously a case anyhow in which you weren't prepared to take sides. Is there anything you would fight for these days? I mean, would you ever get to the stage of saying "I'm going to fight for that!"?

MR. P No, I don't think so.

INTERV. Nothing at all?

MR P. Unless somebody perhaps broke in the house or something like that.

INTERV. I see. It would have to be something very personal before you did it.

MR P. Oh yes. Someone attacking me perhaps. (*He thinks it over.*) Yes.

INTERV. When you were younger did you ever fight? I mean for example were you in the 1914–18 war?

MR P. Yes, I was in the 14–18.

INTERV. And you fought because Kitchener told you to fight, did you?

MR P. I fought for Kitchener, King, and country.

INTERV. Never regretted it?

MR P. No; no we did the right thing then.

INTERV. You think it was a good idea to go to war then?

MR P. Yes, we had to stop them, you know.

INTERV. This is a war as well I would have thought—These boys attacking this conductor—as much a war as 1914–18, although on a smaller scale. Don't you think you should take sides in it? There's an awful lot of this going on, you know and . . . well, you don't know whose side anybody's on. You don't know who's who nowadays, do you? The enemy's rather difficult to see. He doesn't wear a spiked hat and talk German. Because it's like this there's nothing you can do. Is that right?

MR P. (*putting him right in a helpful way*) Of course they didn't wear spiked hats. They wore, you know, the old round things, —tin helmets.

INTERV. In any case, you could recognise one and you can't recognise the enemy today.

MR P. (*obviously not really understanding the point*) Yes, they were different from the English. Yes . . . (*remembering*) They came down over the ears more.

INTERV. And your advice is, "sit tight"?

MR P. Well I think everybody should just go along.

INTERV. (*rather strongly*) What you mean, Mr Phillips, is "sit tight".

MR P. Well, all right, yes.

INTERV. Thank you very much indeed.

Carol and Peter are also in the studio, and as we can see them take their seats another snatch of the incident can be heard.

CAROL You are awful, Peter! You'll do anything like that, won't you?

INTERV. So you two did get married after all, I see from your wedding ring.

PETER   Yes.

CAROL   Yes.

INTERV. Did you ever think you'd break off the engagement when you asked Peter that night to go and do something about the conductor and he didn't?

CAROL   (*very firmly*) Oh, no.

INTERV. You weren't a bit disappointed with his behaviour?

CAROL   Well, I was at the time. I was disappointed at the time, but afterwards when I thought about it sensibly I was glad he didn't get involved.

INTERV. But the conductor got punched up.

CAROL Yes, I know. (*There is a pause as the interviewer looks at her.*) Well, some boys would have got involved, but I can understand why he didn't, because I know him so well.

INTERV. He was brave, was he? Sensible.

CAROL Well, I think he was sensible.

INTERV. Let's talk about the boys on the bus. Do you know them?

CAROL Well, vaguely. One of them lives round the corner to where we live, but we never have anything to do with the family. I mean my mum never talks to their mum.

INTERV. Tell me this: Do you ever feel attracted to that sort of boy? After all he lives a very wild life, he dresses wildly, and he goes about in gangs and makes a lot of noise. Don't you find that sort of boy attractive compared with Peter, who's very quiet?

CAROL Well no, not really, I mean it's all right in moderation, you know flouncing about, but I like Peter because, you know, he's secure.

INTERV. He's your future?

CAROL Yes.

INTERV. How do you want your future to work out?

CAROL Well, a house. We hope to buy one eventually. And a couple of children when we can afford them.

INTERV. Now nobody knows how children are going to turn out. What if your children turned out like those four on the bus?

CAROL Well, I'm going to do all in my power to try and stop that. I'm going to try and bring them up as best I can so they don't feel the need to go around punching up people.

INTERV. Peter, I don't want to embarrass you, but on the bus you didn't in fact do anything to help that conductor who finished in a pretty bad state. Are you sorry about that? Do you think you did right?

PETER I'm not sorry in one way. I just couldn't afford to do anything at that . . .

INTERV. Why not? What do you mean, "afford"?

PETER Well, I was sitting my exams. I had to study. Carol and I

ner, wouldn't you hope that somebody would come and
get you out of it?

DRIVER Yes, I'd hope, but the chances are—(*he fumbles for words*)
it depends on the situation: no one might help me. I wish
I had helped him, but I couldn't.

INTERV. Thank you very much.

Once again we see a section of the incident repeated.

BOY He's paid.

CONDUCT. Has he? Well, where's his ticket then?

BOY He must have dropped it.

CONDUC. Well, where did you drop it?

BOY How do I know?

CONDUC. Look, are you paying?

BOY Twice?

*The final interview is with the conductor who is now in the studio
with the interviewer.*

INTERV. Conductor, how are you feeling?

CONDUC. Oh not too bad. The ribs are still a bit sore you know, and
I had a bad bit of concussion I think, but it's cleared up.

INTERV. It's cleared up?

CONDUC. Yes, I was lucky—I mean compared to the injuries that
some of the boys at the depot have had, you know, in the
past.

INTERV. I see. Tell me about the attitude of the other people on

the bus—the people who didn't come to help you. Do you feel bitter about that?

CONDUC. No, funny, I was just listening. You know, all they seem to do, the whole lot of them, is to make excuses for their own cowardice. I mean one fellow, he hides behind his old age pension book; the other fellow—because he's getting married he didn't want his face messed up; and him because he's a coloured bloke. I mean, you know, well if you're going to sit up there weighing up the pros and cons, all the time . . .

INTERV. That would make me bitter, of course.

CONDUC. Well it does, it makes you angry, because I think if the same thing happened tomorrow, and they were on the bus, they'd probably help tomorrow, now they've had second thoughts.

INTERV. What about the boys though, you must be pretty bitter about them?

CONDUC. Well I would like to know if they had any regrets afterwards. Because really some of those boys, they are not bad boys at heart, you know. I have a young lad.

INTERV. How do you manage to say that? It's very generous, because they punched you up.

CONDUC. Well, no, because I know a young lad that I helped in the past. He had a bit of bother. I helped him. And now he's

at sea. He's on an oil tanker, and he's fine, you know, and
it was very satisfying, knowing that you would help him
and so now I do voluntary work in a youth club, and I
know these types of lads, and given the right opportunities, if they could harness their energy in the right
direction, they'd be all right, you know.

INTERV. I think that's very generous for someone who's been
through what you have been through. One of these lads
called you an "Irish git"?

CONDUC. Yes.

INTERV. So you are an immigrant yourself, aren't you?

CONDUC. Oh, I didn't mind the Irish part of it. I'm proud of that.
But I'm not too happy about the "git" part.

INTERV. Do you feel like an alien?

CONDUC. I feel like a bit of an outsider, I suppose, but I mean there
are so many of us over here now that we are part of the
family.

INTERV. But it's a real English problem, isn't it, this feeling of
separateness? All those people felt separate from each
other, and they felt separate from the boys.

CONDUC. But this always happens in a big city.

INTERV. You think this is a big city problem?

CONDUC. Yes, in the jungle of the big city, you know, where nobody knows anybody, nobody has any identity. I mean a

bus load of people is a bus load of faces. They're here today and gone tomorrow, and who cares?

INTERV. Whereas in a village or a small society . . .

CONDUC. Or a market town where everybody knows the baker, the postman and so on, you come to his assistance, you know. You help one another. But here they don't want to know. I'm not your brother's keeper, you know.

INTERV. So you're a victim of a city problem?

CONDUC. Exactly.

INTERV. Thank you very much.

CONDUC. You're welcome.

We now see one of the boys, Colin, in the studio.

INTERV. And you're one of the four punchers.

COLIN Yes.

INTERV. Sit down, will you? What happened to you after that night. I suppose you got caught. I certainly hope so; did you?

COLIN Yes, one of the girls, she recognised Arthur. That's the one who stole the money like.

INTERV. And what did you get?

COLIN Oh, we went to the Old Bailey, like, and me and Dave, we got six months' detention. Arthur got three months

157

	and old Robbo, that's the big one, he got "six months to two years" [1]Borstal.
INTERV.	What happened in the detention centre?
COLIN	It was a bit rough like. You know, up at half past six in the morning, no smoking. Mind you, you are fit after it.
INTERV.	But you're recovering?
COLIN	Oh, yes.
INTERV.	How did you get yourself into that scrape in the first place? How did you come to be on a bus punching up a conductor?
COLIN	Well, I didn't have much choice really.
INTERV.	I beg your pardon.
COLIN	I didn't have much choice, see.
INTERV.	In what way?
COLIN	Well, it was Robbo; I mean, if I never helped him out he'd have done me over.
INTERV.	I don't understand. You were helping Robbo out, were you?
COLIN	Yes.
INTERV.	He was in trouble was he?
COLIN	Yes.
INTERV.	What sort of trouble?
COLIN	Well, it was that bus conductor like.
INTERV.	What was the bus conductor doing?
COLIN	Well, he put his hand on Robbo, and old Robbo got mad.
INTERV.	You mean that the hand on Robbo was the thing that was enough to make you punch up the bus conductor.
COLIN	It was enough to make Robbo, yes.
INTERV.	And what would have happened if you'd said no?
COLIN	He'd have had me.
INTERV.	Who'd have had you?
COLIN	Robbo
INTERV.	It's like that, is it: You've got this pal, and you go around with him, and yet if you don't do what he says he punches you up?

[1]This is the regular court sentence, allowing the exact length of time to be varied.

COLIN   Yes.

INTERV.   Pretty funny pal, isn't he?

COLIN   It's the way it's always been.

INTERV.   What do you think about the other people on the bus? Do you think of them as human beings, older than you but like you, or do you think . . . they are the enemy, they are the others?

COLIN   Well I don't think of them as the enemy, but I mean nobody can help getting old, can they. It's just the way they look at you, like.

INTERV.   What! Say it again.

COLIN   It's just the way they look at you.

INTERV.   In what way do they look at you?

COLIN   Well, as if you're the freaks or something, just because you've got long hair and all that.

INTERV.   And that worries you enough to make you punch them up?

COLIN   Yes.

INTERV.   Have you been in trouble with the police before?

COLIN   Yes. I've been 'ad up for thieving.

INTERV.   When was that?

COLIN   Oh, I used to work at a garage and I used to pocket the money, like, and the guv'nor found out and got the law on me. I got probation.

INTERV. Got probation, and that wasn't enough to warn you off. You still went in and started punching up. What about school? Did you enjoy it?

COLIN No.

INTERV. Where did you sit in the class?

COLIN At the back.

INTERV. Why?

COLIN I don't know. I just weren't bothered.

INTERV. What would have happened if some other kid had tried to get to the back row when you wanted it?

COLIN It depends who he was, like.

INTERV. If he was bigger than you?

COLIN Well, I'd think twice about it.

INTERV. And if he wasn't bigger than you?

COLIN Well, I would have had him.

INTERV. You would have punched him?

COLIN Yes.

INTERV. I see. What about the future then? Is it going to go on like this in a cycle of getting into trouble, getting probation or a prison sentence, coming out, having a good time and going in again? Is it going to go on like this?

COLIN Well, I'd like to sort of get a steady job but I don't see many people giving me the chance, once they know I've been inside, like.

INTERV. I think you're saying that before you know. I mean the first thing probably is to get rid of Robbo, isn't it?

COLIN Well, it's all right for you to say it, I mean you're all right, but I mean a fellow like me, I've been inside; I know what it's like. I know what it's like when you come out and try to get a normal job.

INTERV. What's the solution, then?

COLIN Well, it depends if you're lucky, you know—if I can sort of lie about it.

INTERV. Lie about being in prison?

COLIN Yes.

INTERV. I don't think that's a solution.

COLIN It's the only way I can think out of it.

INTERV. I suggest perhaps while Robbo's inside as he is for a bit, isn't he?, you might get this opportunity to find a job do you think?

COLIN   Yes, well I'll have a go like, you know.

INTERV. But you're not very hopeful.

COLIN   No, I ain't.

INTERV. Thank you very much..

The interviewer turns to the camera

We know a bit more about the hopes and fears of the people who happened to be travelling on that bus that night. What those people said really leaves us with three questions: Who was to blame for what happened on the bus that night? And secondly, is there anything that can be done to stop it happening again? Not just on that bus, but anywhere?

We see him in close-up for the end of the programme.

What do you think?

Producing "£60 Single, £100 Return"

by Ronald Smedley *Senior Producer, BBC School Television and director of this and other plays in the volume.*

The script

You can't start a play without a script, and there is no point in starting without a good one. When Bill Lyons sent me the script of "*£60 Single, £100 Return*" I liked it very much: I thought it was interesting; I wanted to know what happened next and the things the people were saying seemed real and lifelike. I laughed at some of the conversation at Des's home and I felt sorry for Pete and his mother. Not that the script that Bill sent at first was the one I finally accepted. For example, the original scene in the café seemed far too long in getting to the point: Desmond came across the advertisement by chance half way through the scene, not having thought about it before. Can you see what changes I suggested and why? Were they just to save time?

But the biggest change from the first script to the final play comes in the last scene at Des's house. This was what Pete said originally:

PETE Des, I'm not coming.

DES Yer what?

PETE I can't . . . I'm not coming to India.

DES Just like that?

PETE No, not just like that. You know how my mum keeps going on at me. She keeps making out she'll never see me again if I go and . . . well she's getting on a bit and she's always done a lot for me.

So, in fact, Pete has given in to his mother. The last shot is of Desmond ringing up the travel agent.

DES Whatever Pete said doesn't go for me. I'm still going to India.

But Bill changed the whole play. After we talked about it he made the decision that the wrong boy was going to India. So he rewrote a great deal. How has that changed the characters of Des and Peter? Has it made it a better story?

There were a lot more changes in the script, right up until rehearsals were under way, but those were the two most important ones. Would you, for instance, like to make Pete different, his mother different, Des's father different—and, if so, why?

Getting cracking

I accepted the final version of the play. Now I started to plan the campaign of producing it. I decided not to use any film shot outside in the streets, in real cafés or real houses, but to create the whole play in a television studio, which would mean designing and building three sets: the café, Pete's house and Des's house. Pete's house needs a living-room and a kitchen; Des's house needs a backyard as well as a living-room and an entrance hall for the phone call. The café doesn't need to be very large. So I sent the designer the script, and when he'd had a chance to read it through we met and talked about it. So far as design goes this play is not a difficult one; it doesn't require anything very complicated or unusual, but the sets must be convincing—after all everybody knows what living-rooms, back yards, and cafés look like. The other problem is that the scenery must fit comfortably into the studio and give me enough room to move my cameras about and get the pictures I need. It's no good designing attractive and convincing sets that will leave no room for the cameras.

On page 165 you can see a bird's eye view of the studio, Studio five at the Television Centre; the designer and I will draw a plan of the sets and the camera positions onto a larger version of this bird's eye view. Everything will be to scale: each square on the drawing represents a square foot in the studio. On pages 166 and 167 you can see a *simplified* version of *part* of this studio plan with the set of Pete's house and the café drawn in. You can see the way in which cameras one, two, three and four look *into* the sets. A means the first position for a camera and B means the second. C and D (not shown) will mean the third and fourth as necessary. I have not drawn in the microphone positions; they are usually shown.

Choosing the actors

People often ask how you choose actors for a play: there are several ways. I know quite a number of actors (and actresses) already from having seen plays on the stage and television and having produced other plays myself. If I see a good performance from someone I try to make a note of it and remember it for the future so that, when I read a play and think of casting I can say to myself, "I can see so and so playing that part". Let's take the two boys, Pete and Des. Pete is quiet and sensitive, nice to his mother, and able to put up with a lot of pushing around; Des is noisy, boisterous and good for a laugh. I thought I knew exactly who I wanted to play these two parts, Simon Ward and Roy Holder. In a way, Simon and Roy are not unlike Pete and Des in themselves. But that doesn't mean to say that you must always look for an actor who is the spitting image of the part he has to play. Many good actors can play all sorts of parts, not just parts that reflect their own character and physique. A good actor is a sensitive intelligent person who can read a play and say of a part: "I think I understand that person; I think I know why he behaves like he does. I think I can bring him to life."

I rang Simon's and Roy's agents (most actors have agents who look after them) and the two boys read the script. The agents agreed on a fee and the boys accepted. In the same way I "contacted" Jean Boht, Ken

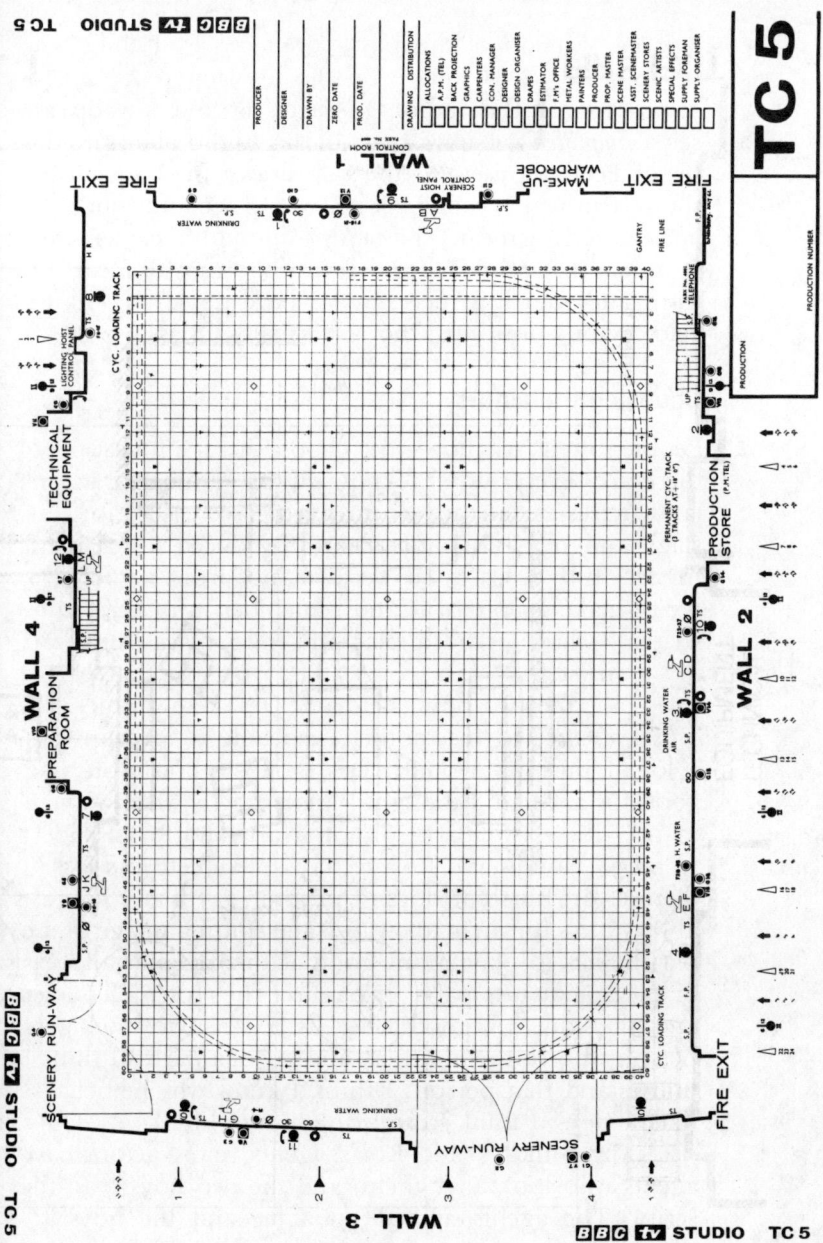

BBC tv STUDIO TC 5

TC 5

FIRE EXIT

WALL 1

MAKE-UP
WARDROBE

FIRE EXIT

WALL 2

PRODUCTION
STORE (P.K.TEL)

GANTRY

FIRE LINE

PRODUCTION NUMBER

PRODUCTION

CYC. LOADING TRACK

PERMANENT CYC. TRACK
(3 TRACKS AT + 4')

WALL 4

TECHNICAL
EQUIPMENT

PREPARATION
ROOM

SCENERY RUN-WAY

BBC tv STUDIO TC 5

LIGHTING HOIST
CONTROL PANEL

CYC. LOADING TRACK

SCENERY RUN-WAY

WALL 3

BBC tv STUDIO TC 5

165

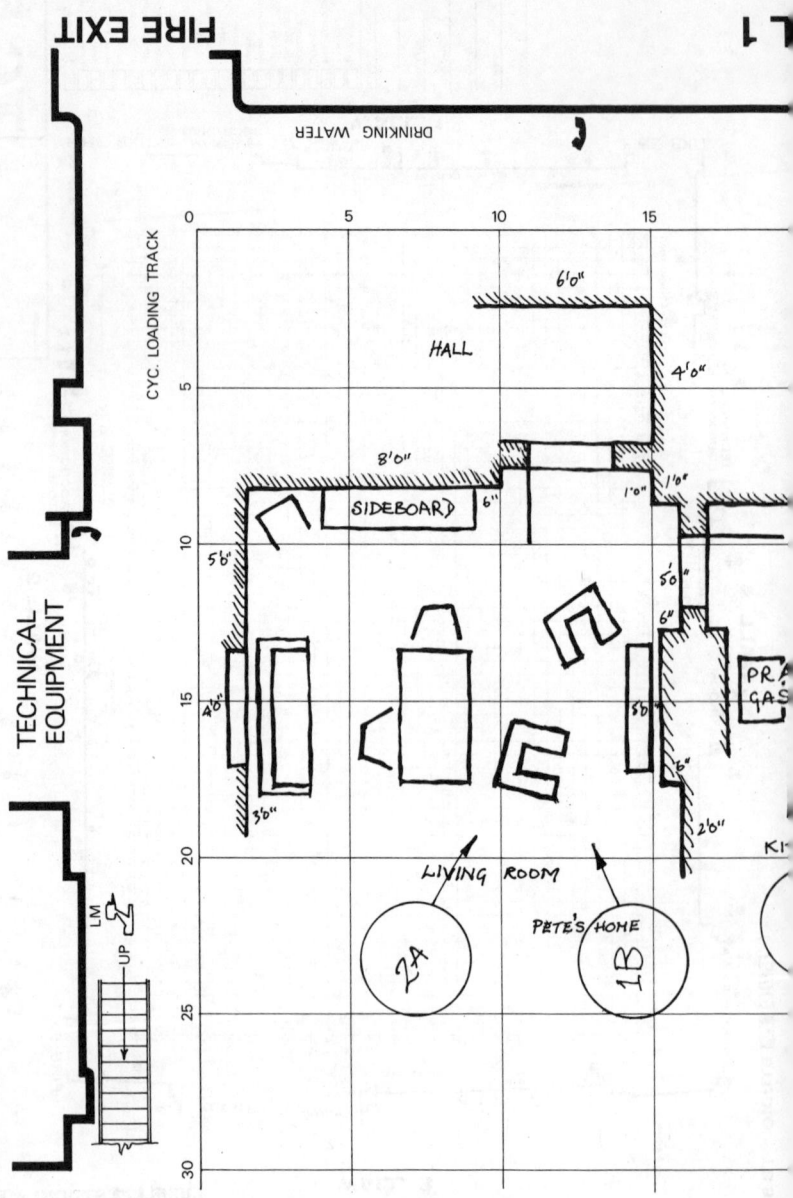

FIRE EXIT

DRINKING WATER

TECHNICAL
EQUIPMENT

UP
LM

CYC. LOADING TRACK

0   5   10   15

6'0"

HALL

4'0"

8'0"

SIDEBOARD   6"

1'0"   1'0"

5'6"

5'0"

6"

4'0"

5'6"

6"

3'6"

2'6"

PR
GAS

KI

LIVING ROOM

PETE'S HOME

2A

1B

166

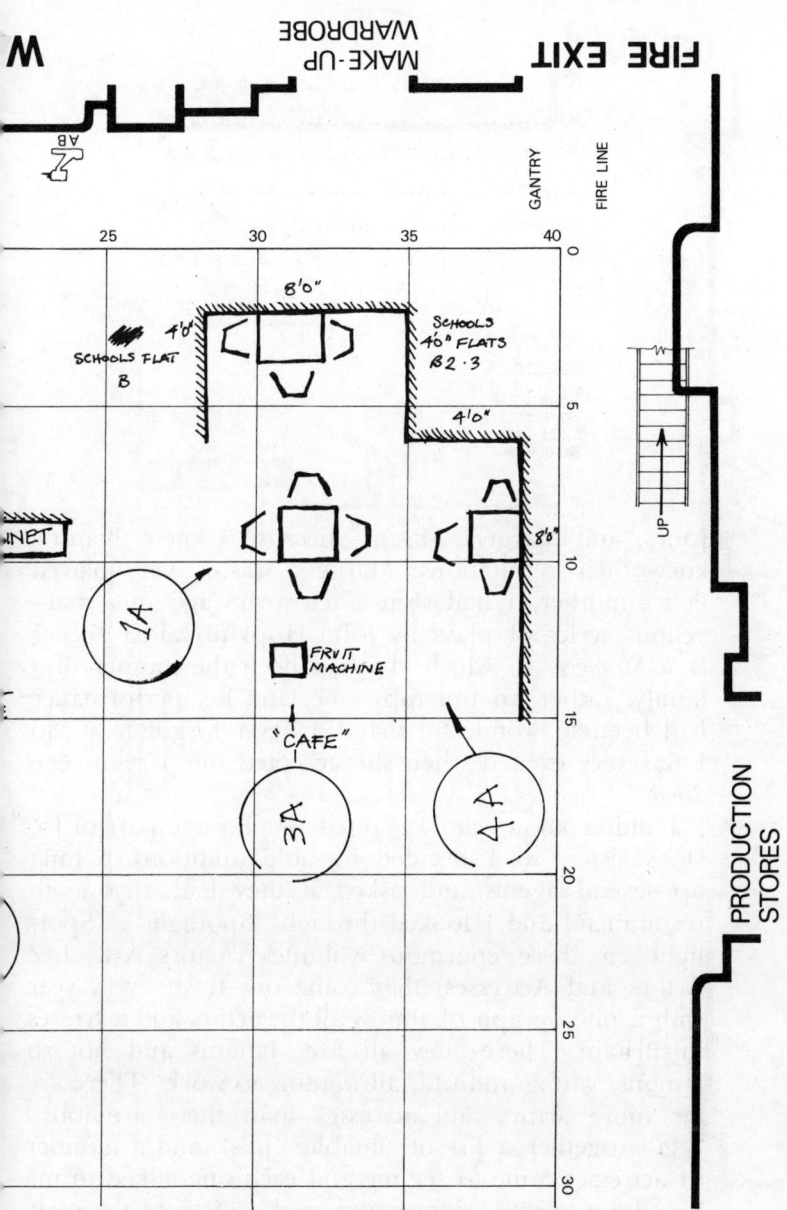

CAST LIST

PETE	SIMON WARD
DES	ROY HOLDER
MRS. BRAY	MARGERY MASON
MR. POTTER	KEN JONES
MRS. POTTER	JEAN BOHT
JO	SALLY FAULKNER

Walk-ons

GRACE DOLAN
REX RASHLEY
LINDA OXER
BRIAN KING

Jones, and Margery Mason—because I knew them or knew their reputations. Margery Mason, who played Pete's mother, I had seen a few years ago in a marvellous series of plays by John Hopkins called *Talking to a Stranger*, in which she had been the mother of a family, rather an unhappy one, and her performance had been so wonderful that I'd never forgotten it. So I was very excited when she accepted the part in *£60 Single*.

I didn't know who I wanted to play the part of Jo, Des's sister, so I decided to hold auditions. I rang up several agents and asked if they had anyone to recommend and I looked through "Spotlight". "Spotlight" is three enormous volumes (Actors A-K, L-Z Actors and Actresses) that come out fresh every year with a photograph of almost all the actors and actresses in Britain. There they all are, famous and not so famous, young and old, all wanting to work. (There are far more actors and actresses than there are jobs.) I got together a list of suitable "Jo's" and a number of actresses came to see me and each one talked to me for about twenty minutes and read a piece of the play.

After all this I chose Sally Faulkner to play the part. Auditions are difficult: it's not easy to judge on one meeting whether the person you're chatting to or listening to can really become the person in the play. And sometimes you find several people who might do. If the part is large or very important you might have to see the actors more than once or even look at them through a camera or on film, because if a good script is vital so are the right actors. And, of course, auditions are often nerve-racking things for the actors and you may not always see the real personality at the audition. I remember once casting for a play, not one in this book, where I was looking for a teenager to play the part of an apprentice in a factory. A young actor came to see me—he strolled in as if he owned the place, chewing gum, making cheeky remarks and behaving in such a way that you were forced to think to yourself, "I'd never have that lad in the cast. He'd drive us all mad." I thanked him for coming but just as he was leaving I saw that his hands were shaking like a leaf and he could hardly hold the door handle. As I actually had liked his reading I cast him: he was smashing and everybody liked him very much. He was just very shy.

So we had a cast and we were ready to go. The play lasts nearly half an hour, and that takes about a week to rehearse and a day in the studio to record. (Like most plays we were going to record it for transmission later.)

The rehearsals

The first day of rehearsal arrives and we all meet together for the first time. We have a cup of coffee, sit down around a large table and have what's called a "read through". On p. 170 we are "reading through" in the middle of a large rehearsal room. This is not the studio where the play will eventually be recorded—studios are too fully booked for that—but a special room in a large block of rehearsal rooms. Already the assistant floor manager has been in

Top left: The read through. *Top right*: The producer and author at the read through. *Bottom left*: An early stage of rehearsal. From left to right, assistant floor manager, producer, Simon (Pete) and Margery (Mum), talking about moves in the make-believe Pete's house: 'stove' in the foreground and Pete's dining-room. *Bottom right*: The producer discussing a point in rehearsal.

for several hours and marked out the floor. That means that all the outlines of the rooms in Pete's house, Des's house and the café have been marked on the floor with sticky tapes. The door openings are marked with poles and the rooms have been filled with old bits of furniture, make-believe gas stoves, cardboard fruit machines and a fairy cycle standing in for the motorbike. The "real" walls, gas stove and motorbike arrive in the studio only on the recording day.

When the read through has ended, and the ice has been broken (because even actors can be quite shy, like most people, on meeting for the first time) the next stage of the rehearsal begins.

I must already have sat down with the script and the designer's plans and know how the actors are going to move around (or stay still) when they're saying their lines. What sort of things do people do when they're at home or in a café? Do they stand up, sit down, cook the dinner, drum their fingers or what? So I've had to sort out my idea of "the moves" in my mind's eye before we start and very slowly, making notes on their script, the actors write down the moves I suggest and find their way about the make-believe rooms.

For instance, before Pete comes home in Scene 2 we see Mum first of all. Now she's obviously houseproud, fussy, hard-working; she doesn't sit and watch the telly much. She'd be tidying up after her unseen grandson's visit, and when Peter comes in we've got to feel that his mother is over-protecting him—after all, that's part of the trouble isn't it? So we gave Mrs Bray lots of things to do, out to the kitchen for his tea from the oven, back again for the afters. Not too much of course; this is a serious play, not a farce where everything is exaggerated. But Mrs Bray doesn't sit down at all; it's Pete who's quiet and does little except be looked after. Can you see how that helps? Of course the actors will have lots of ideas of their own as well.

Now that moves are plotted, we get down to the next stage of finding out what it's all about, what it really means. And this means a lot of discussing between all the cast and myself. What does Peter really think about his mother, why do Des's parents react to the news in the way they do? We keep trying things out, changing a bit, sometimes changing a lot—from the way words are said, to the actual words themselves. The actors, even though they still have their scripts in their hands, are "trying out" their parts, developing a relationship with each other. Now it's a very odd thing to be an actor—you are yourself and yet you're not. Just like a painter or a musician you're creating something—but instead of a painting or a piece of music—you're creating another person with yourself and that other person is going to be looked at by thousands, perhaps (on TV) by millions of people. And if it's not right or unconvincing—you'll be blamed. How ter-

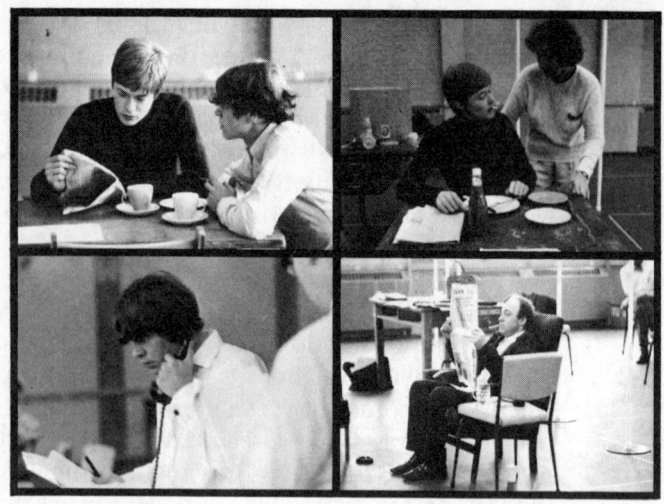

Top left: Simon (Pete) and Roy (Des) at 'café' table. *Top right*: Rehearsing the meal in scene 2: Simon (Pete) and Margery (Mum). *Bottom left*: In rehearsal: Roy (Des) with script, 'phone' and pencil. *Bottom right*: Ken Jones (Mr Potter) in the Potters' front room, waiting for his scene to start. *Below*: Sally (Jo) and Roy (Des) in rehearsal, with 'motorbike'

rible if everybody laughed when they weren't supposed to, or were embarrassed by a bad performance or switched off and wrote to the papers. So an actor has to develop his part, even quite a simple one, very carefully in rehearsals and in an atmosphere where he can trust people not to laugh at him—of course—but also where he can trust people, the director in particular, to say "that's good, that'll work" or "that's not quite so good; there's probably a better way of doing that". There's got to be an atmosphere at a rehearsal where an actor feels two things —that nobody minds when they try things out and that the director knows whether what they're trying is right or wrong.

Soon the scripts are put aside and the rehearsals get further and further ahead, and people get more and more sure of themselves. Now I must start to plan the "electronic" part of the production—how I'm going to use my four cameras when I get into the studio.

The cameras

I've got to plan to use the cameras in such a way that the play comes over clearly and is interesting to look at. So now I must sit down and plan the shots. Let's take the scene where Mr Potter is talking to Des about the fact that Des has lost his evening job (page 13). I could just take a camera, plonk it down in front of the Potters' living room, and let you see everything that goes on. But how much better it would be if we looked only at the things we really wanted to see, the things that really make the story come alive.

So let's see what I've done with my cameras in a part of one particular scene. It's very simple. It's described on what is called the camera script, page 21 of which is shown on the following page.

On the left-hand side of the script the picture or visuals are described and on the right the sounds. Let's start at 118. This means shot 118—the 118th "picture"

118. 1 C 2-S DES AND MRS. POTTER	POTTER: I was in the pub last night. /
119. 4 C MCU MR. POTTER	DES: That's not news.
120. 3 C ~~MCU~~ DES CU	POTTER: Mate of mine told me that you'd lost that evening job in the factory. Late once too often he said. Some old story, just like that other job he lost. MRS. POTTER: Is this true Des? DES: Well ..... JO: So you haven't got the money to go.
121. 4 C MCU MR. POTTER	DES: I'll raise it somehow. /
122. 3 C MCU DES	POTTER: There is one way you could. /
123. 4 C MCU MR. POTTER	DES: Oh yeh? /
124. 1 C CU ~~2-S DES & MRS POTTER~~	POTTER: Yeh. You could sell that bloody Jumbo jet out in the yard there and then maybe we'll all get some peace. /
125. 4 C MCU MR. POTTER	DES: What, my bike after all the work I've put in on it. /
126. 1 C MCU DES HOLD his rise PAN down to MRS. POTTER PAN MRS. POTTER to window	POTTER: It's the only way you'll raise the money in the time. So it depends how much you want to go doesn't it. / DES: All right then! If I have to .... if it's the only way. I will, if it's the only way. DES GOES OUT INTO YARD /
127. 4 C MCU MRS. POTTER	

(128 on 3)

of the programme. Shot one was the title of the play, shot two was a "picture" of the fruit machine in the café and shot three was Pete reading the paper. So every time we move from one picture (or shot) to another we add a number—and everyone knows where they are. Shot 118 comes from Camera 1 in position c looking into the Potters' living room). Now look below the line of shot 118 on the script: the cameraman will understand from what I've written—"2-S Des & Mrs Potter"—that 118 is a "two shot", a shot of two people, Desmond and his mother. On the right-hand side you can see that Des is speaking. Then there's a line to show that I intend to cut to another camera—camera 4 in C position in the Potters' living room. This will be shot 119. Look below the line. Mr Potter is speaking. What he is saying is important: we find out more about Desmond's character in Mr Potter's speech so I go close to Mr Potter's face to get the full force of his words. I describe the shot as MCU—a medium close up. All we see is Mr Potter's head and shoulders. I'm also very interested in what effect Dad's words are having on Des so before Mr Potter has finished speaking I cut to camera 3 (C position) and look at Des. You can see from the script that I changed my mind and I've crossed out MCU and written CU instead— a close up. This will show me only Desmond's face. I changed the shot because Desmond is quite upset at being found out, and the nearer to his face we are the more apparent this is. If you're found out you don't do much. Practise looking "found out" in a mirror—see what I mean? It's just something to do with the eyes.

Of course the camera doesn't need to be about two inches from Desmond's face to get a CU. The cameramen has four lenses to choose from, mounted on the front of his camera. If he selects the right one, this gives a closer picture almost without moving the camera at all. Now I expect you can work out the rest of the page. I altered shot 124 as you can see. That was because the shot of Des and his mother was difficult for camera one to get without giving me an "ugly" picture so I changed it. Look at shot 126: this is a bit more complicated. This starts MCU Des but then Des gets up and leaves the room, so I've decided that the camera keeps looking at Des as he gets up—"hold his rise", and as he leaves, because Mum's a bit upset, the camera moves down or pans down to see Mum and then goes across with her to the window—"pans her to the window".

This is a very simple page of camera script. Nobody moves around very much and there aren't any close-ups of Mum's knitting or Dad's glass of beer which we might have needed to tell the story. Of course shots should also be good to look at as well as telling the story. So that's the camera script done: thirty pages and two hundred and five shots typed out.

Back to the rehearsal

Look at these photos, here we are still in the rehearsal room but we've been "invaded" by all the chief technicians who are going to control the lights, the microphones and the cameras, when we get into the studio. They are standing watching the rehearsal, with floor plans in their hands, making sure they know what the actors do, where they stand, how they move, so that they can plan how best to light the sets, place the microphones—and also to tell me if I've worked out anything in rehearsal that won't work in the studio, like putting an actor where he can't be properly lit or seen.

Now we're nearly ready. The designer has made the sets and hired the furnishings and fittings; he's rented a pin-table machine and a motorbike for the day and gone through all the fine details that must be there to bring the play to life. The costume supervisor has chosen the clothes the actors will wear. Now we run the play through several times without any stops or pauses until the actors really feel, not only that they know but that they understand the play and understand each other.

Above and below left: The technicians, with floor plans, make notes during rehearsal. *Above right*: The scene being rehearsed in the Potters' house

Think how important it is for Margery and Simon to be able to feel that they really are mother and son in that rather strained home; they've got to be able to feel that they've lived in the make-believe house for a long time and that there are all sorts of things they know about each other, just as in any family, that's not in the script of the play. So these last "run throughs" are very quiet affairs, where no one speaks or moves around unless they're in the play and we *all* concentrate together on getting the play understood. A director must be right there, looking and watching every second, to make sure as best he can that all's going well, and also to be the *audience*, to be for the time being the person the actors are acting to.

The recording

Then comes the big day. It's going to be a hard day for us all. We start at 10.00 a.m. and don't finish till 10.00 p.m. All the time, apart from meal breaks, we're in the brightly lit studio five, at BBC's Television Centre. This is a small studio but big enough for what we want to do. The scenery will have been set the previous evening and at 8.30 the senior electrician and his assistants will start to "light" the set, using the special TV lights that hang in great clusters from the ceiling. Then about 9.30 the cameras and the microphones are rolled out of the store room, the cables are plugged in and at 10.30 sharp I go in to the control room above the studio and we begin the camera rehearsal. We all have camera scripts to work from and very slowly we begin to work to put together, like a jig-saw puzzle, all the shots that I have planned. This must be done carefully but we have very little time and woe betide me if my planning hasn't been very good and the shots don't work or the cameras can't see what I want them to see.

I rarely go down to the studio floor. In fact I hardly see the cast at all that day. I sit and look at the four monitor screens in front of me in the control room. Each screen shows the picture that each one of the four cameras can offer me. We sort each shot out till it seems right and then, when we've looked through a whole scene of shots (perhaps the forty-two shots that make up the first scene in the café) we try to run all the shots together, one after the other, one to forty-two! On my right sits a girl, the vision mixer: she has buttons and levers in front of her and it's she who actually cuts from one camera to the other and "chooses" the one we shall look at (according to the script of course) at any one time. This is a very skilled job. She has to judge just the exact moment when to cut,

From left to right, top to bottom: The studio, looking on to the floor through the lights; A cameraman; The gallery with, from right to left, engineer, vision mixer, producer and secretary; The studio beyond seen from the gallery; The producer and intercom microphone; Monitor sets in the gallery. No 4 camera chosen, in C position; The vision mixer; The vision mixer's buttons and knobs.

and it's not always on an easy thing like the end of a sentence; sometimes it's the turn of a head, or a door opening just a certain amount—and she's also got to watch with one eye at the camera she's coming to next— if it's not ready, not quite there, or a fraction out of focus she mustn't cut. If she does it's her fault. Shots come thick and fast in a play, and of everybody in the gallery she has to have perhaps the clearest head and the nimblest fingers.

By teatime we should have worked through everything and made all the small changes we need, like changing a shot from an MCU to CU. We are ready to do a complete run through or rehearsal without stops. I try to have two of these. This is as much for the cameramen who have a lot of fast moving to do as for the actors—but we all need it.

We have supper and then it happens. All that work and money and worry are going to the test. The video tape recording machine stands by in the basement of the TV Centre and at 8.30 p.m. precisely we begin. The vision mixer stands by. I speak if necessary over a little microphone to the earphones of the cameramen and the recording goes ahead. This is a very tense time for everybody and I always feel a bit sick before we start. You can imagine how the actors feel: all the training has been for this one performance, they have to hit the mark now or it's all been wasted. Of course, as the programme is recorded, we can, up to a point, retake scenes or shots that don't work. The café scene we took twice because it didn't have the "life" it could have had the first time. Des's motorbike refused to start (we'd forgotten to switch the petrol on). In the last scene, quite a tense one, Des fell over a bucket and Pete, try as he would, couldn't help laughing.

But by nearly ten o'clock the recording was finished and the engineer in charge of the recording machine was satisfied and we had a "clear" from the senior engineer. At once the scenery started to come down, the cameras were quickly stored away and it was all over— waiting for the audience to see and, we hope, to enjoy.

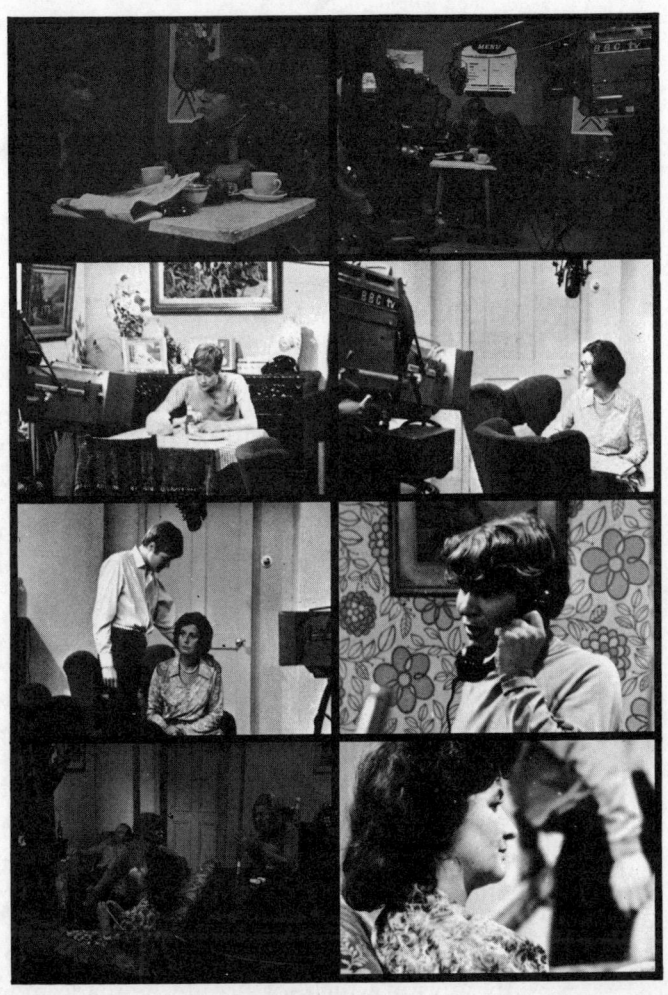

From left to right, top to bottom: What the viewer sees, and how a studio visitor would see it; Pete on the studio floor; In Pete's house; Pete and Mum on the studio floor; Compare this with the rehearsal photo on page 172; The Potters' house; Camera 4 panning from Des to Mum

Talking Points

"£60 Single, £100 Return"

1 Does Mrs Bray fuss too much over Pete?
2 Which family would you rather live in?
3 Des obviously doesn't think much of his sister. What is your opinion of her?
4 Which of the two boys has the stronger character?
5 Why do the boys want to go to India? Do many people of their age feel they'd like a holiday like this?

Terry

1 "Being happy, that's what counts!" says Terry. Is it? Are his hopes possible or unreasonable?
2 What do you think of Maitland? Is he wasting his time doing this job? How much help can adults give young people in finding their jobs?
3 Do you blame Janie for ditching Terry?
4 "That's not settling down. That's blackmail!"—another of Terry's objections to what is expected of him. Is he right to fear "settling down"?
5 Are many jobs as bad as Terry thinks? Are many people as dissatisfied with them as Terry? Are there any ways in which jobs could be made more interesting?

Hero in the dust

1 Is Mick entirely to blame for his anti-social behaviour? If not, who else is also partly to blame?
2 Who had sent for the police?

3 Did Barney handle Mick in a sensible way?
4 Is there usually some "excuse" for people like Mick?
   What, if anything, should people do to help them?
5 Do youth clubs do any good for trouble-makers?

It's me—Eileen

1 Are Eileen's parents reasonable or too strict with her?
   Are there any other reasons why Eileen should want to
   move?
2 Do many young men or women live away from home
   before they marry? What are the arguments for and
   against this?
3 What will Eileen do next, do you think? If she goes
   home, how will her parents behave?
4 What is your impression of Deana?
5 Is there bound to be trouble between young people
   and their parents while they are still at home, or can
   they live happily together?

Clean sweep

1 Do people like Watson often do well for themselves,
   or get in difficulties in the end?
2 When it comes to practical work how valuable is the
   kind of education that Gregg is good at?
3 Is Mr Collett going about his new responsibility in a
   sensible way?
4 What would you feel and do if you were a man working
   in this particular factory?

Time hurries on

1 Do you think Tony was honest, or was he tricking
   Barbara?
2 Will Barbara be any different after this?
3 How typical do you think Mrs Patterson's experience
   is?

4 Are early marriages more likely to fail than later ones? If so, why?

Last bus

1 Would you have helped the bus conductor if you had been on the bus?
2 Who is to blame for the boys' behaviour? The boys themselves, their families, the school they came from, or society more generally?
3 Is there any way by which conductors or others doing public jobs like this can be protected?
4 How do the other passengers seem to you to show up in the interviewing?
5 Is the interviewer fair to them in his questioning?
6 Should these boys be punished? If so, how?

The Authors

Michael Cahill

Michael Cahill was born of Irish-Jewish parentage in Soho in 1930. At the age of three his family moved into the East End of London. He grew up there, experiencing the tough street life, until the outbreak of the second world war; when he was evacuated to the village of Aston Clinton in Buckinghamshire. He left school at fourteen and returned to London to work. He attended the Toynbee Hall Institute for further education during the evenings and did a variety of jobs from labouring to office work and window dressing, until he sold his first play to BBC-TV in 1958. He was commissioned to write more and then wrote for the ITV Companies as well. He has written three major series for Thames Television Schools which received wide acclaim, and is at present working on a film scenario.

Keith Dewhurst

Keith Dewhurst was born in Oldham in 1931; he went to Rydal School, Colwyn Bay, and then on to Cambridge University. He worked for a time in a cotton mill, and later was for some time a reporter with Kemsley Newspapers in Manchester. During much of this time he was a travelling reporter with the Manchester United football team, and covered the 1958 world cup with them. Since 1959 he has been a freelance television writer. He has written many *Z Cars* plays, including *Birds of the Air* and *Running Milligan* (in the *Z Cars* volume in this series), and a play for schools television specially commissioned by the BBC: *The Life of Karen Gillhooly*. His first stage play, *Rafferty's*

Chant, was produced at the Mermaid Theatre, London, in 1967.

Rex Edwards

Rex Edwards was born during the First World War, the son of a policeman. He worked in social service for several years as warden of the Oxford Community Centre and Community Centres Officer for Middlesex before becoming a full time writer.

He has written over ninety episodes of *Dixon of Dock Green* and scripts for *The Avengers*, *No Hiding Place* and *Z Cars*. He spent five years as a member of *The Dales* writing team.

Ronald Eyre

Ronald Eyre was born in Yorkshire in 1929. After serving in the Air Force he went to University College, Oxford, where he was secretary of the Oxford University Dramatic Society, acting in many Oxford productions and making a tour of the USA. After Oxford, Ronald Eyre became an English teacher, first at Queen Elizabeth Grammar School, Blackburn, and then at Bromsgrove School.

He is a modest person, who rather dislikes being caught up in the system of a career. He has himself said that he "signed off from life at the age of six", and that he "didn't really wake up until he was thirty".

In 1956 he joined the BBC schools television department as a drama producer, and for eight years directed the schools drama programmes, which included plays as varied as *The Caucasian Chalk Circle*, *Julius Caesar*, *The Queen and the Rebels*, and the first version of *Clean Sweep*, which he wrote specially for the series. Towards the end of this time Ronald Eyre directed a number of plays for the normal evening programmes, including *The Fire Raisers* and *As you Like It*, and an episode for the *Z Cars* series, which he wrote himself, *Window Dressing* (included in the *Z Cars* volume in Longman Imprint Books). He has written a number of television plays, one of which, *A Crack in the Ice*, he later adapted for the stage. More recently Ronald Eyre has also directed a number of plays in the theatre, including ones for the Royal Shakespeare Company and the National Theatre.

Bill Lyons

Bill Lyons was sixteen when he first acted professionally. When he was twenty-three he wrote his first play—for radio, and since then he has written a number more, including *Elegy for a Comb and Paper Band* and *Such Quantities of Sand*. He still, however, spends most of his time acting, and has, for instance appeared in a number of television series, including *Z Cars*.

Alan Plater

Alan Plater started to write whilst still in his teens. He was born in Jarrow-on-Tyne, but his family moved to Hull when he was three. When he left Kingston High School, Hull, he went to King's College, Newcastle, to study architecture, which he saw, as he puts it, as a "respectable alternative to ivory towers". After two years in an architect's office in Hull ("the only real job I've ever had"), he became a full-time writer when his first play, *The Smoke Zone*, was broadcast on the radio in 1961.

Sound radio gave him his first opportunities, and eight of his plays have been produced including *Mating Season* (included in the volume *Worth a Hearing*, in Blackie's Student Drama series). Alan Plater has written an even larger number of plays for television, including *A Smashing Day*, *So-Long Charlie*, and the *Nutter*. The *Z Cars* series was of especial interest to him, and the script in this volume was one of eighteen which he wrote for the series.

The live theatre, particularly when closely attached to a particular region, interests Alan Plater most. The

Victoria Theatre, Stoke-on-Trent has produced many of his stage plays, including *Teds' Cathedral*. This theatre has grown out of *local* interest, and Alan Plater feels strongly that the arts flourish most valuably in a regional setting so that each region needs an Arts Centre. He is deeply involved in schemes for such a centre in his own city, Hull.

Fay Weldon

Fay Weldon's plays frequently appear on television: between 1966 and 1970 fifteen of her plays were shown. She has also contributed episodes to many series, including *Kate, Upstairs, Downstairs* and *Suspicion*, and has published two novels, *The Fat Woman's Joke* and *Down Amongst the Women*. Before she was able to take up full-time writing she worked in advertising, where she coined the slogan "Go to work on an egg".

A Choice of Books

In reading, one title leads on to another, and we often find most pleasure in picking up a book which in some way or other has been prompted by what we have just read and enjoyed. Listed here is a small choice of books which in various ways touch on similar experiences and ideas to those of the plays in this collection. It would be especially good for members of a group working with this collection each to read a different book from this list and to compare notes later. Groups working on dramatic improvisations or creating their own plays or stories after reading these television scripts will also find the following books helpful comparisons and starting points.

Stories

BANKS, LYN REID, *The L-Shaped Room* Chatto and Windus
BARSTOW, STAN, *A Kind of Loving* Hutchinson
BARSTOW, STAN, *Joby*, Bodley Head
BEHAN, BRENDAN, *Borstal Boy*, Hutchinson
CHAPLIN, SID, *The Leaping Lad*, Longman (*Imprint Books*)
CLEARY, BEVERLY, *Fifteen*, Heinemann
DRABBLE, MARGARET, *The Millstone*, Longman (*Imprint Books*)
DYMENT, CLIFFORD, *The Railway Game*, Dent
HANLEY, CLIFFORD, *A Taste of Too Much*, Blackie
KAMM, JOSEPHINE, *Young Mother*, Heinemann
MARLAND, EILEEN and MICHAEL, editors, *Friends and Families*, Longman (*Imprint Books*)
MARLAND, MICHAEL, editor. *The Experience of Work*, Longman (*Imprint Books*)
MOODY, H.L.B., *Facing Facts*, Blackie

NAUGHTON, BILL, *Late Night on Watling Street*, Longman (*Imprint Books*)

NAUGHTON, BILL, *One Small Boy*, Longman (*Imprint Books*)

ROWE, ALBERT, *People Like You*, Faber

SILLITOE, ALAN, *A Sillitoe Selection*, Longman (*Imprint Books*)

SILLITOE, ALAN, *The Loneliness of the Long-Distance Runner*, Longman (*Heritage of Literature*)

WATERHOUSE, KEITH, *Billy Liar*, Longman (*Imprint Books*)

UNWIN, G. G., editor, *A Taste for Living*, Faber

WRIGHT, RICHARD, *Black Boy*, Longman (*Imprint Books*)

Plays

BARSTOW, STAN, and BRADLEY, ALFRED, *A Kind of Loving*, Blackie

DELANEY, SHELAGH, *A Taste of Honey*, Methuen

MARLAND, MICHAEL, editor, *Theatre Choice*, Blackie

RECKFORD, BARRY, *Skyvers*, Penguin

TERSON, PETER, *Zigger-Zagger*, Penguin

WATERHOUSE, KEITH and HALL, WILLIS, *Billy Liar*, Blackie

Television scripts

GALTON, ALAN and SIMPSON, RAY, *Hancock's Half Hour*, Evans, *Steptoe and Son*, Longman (*Imprint Books*)

HOPKINS, JOHN, *Talking to a Stranger*, Penguin

MARLAND, MICHAEL, editor, *Z Cars*, Longman (*Imprint Books*)

MARLAND, MICHAEL, editor, *Conflicting Generations*, Longman (*Imprint Books*)

MANVELL, ROGER, *The July Plot*, Blackie

OWEN, ALUN, *Three Televison Plays*, Cape

OWEN, ALUN, *The Wake* in *Theatre Choice*, Blackie

A Note for Teachers

This volume has been devised from the well tried and successful BBC Schools Television series *Scene*, which has been running now since 1968. In the words of the producer, the programmes in *Scene* are "meant to contribute to the study of the humanities, in its broadest sense, in the middle school (aged 14–16). They are meant to stimulate discussion and an exploration of topics which have a general and, in some cases, highly personal relevance to the situation of young people today".

The series is rare in using both documentary programmes and specially written plays: seven of these have been chosen here. It is important to stress what a reading will anyway make clear: these scripts are not mere "dramatised documentaries", but real plays in which the authors' feelings for their characters and their situations come across powerfully. Each of the scripts chosen was well received by pupil audiences when transmitted, and each reads well in the classroom. Although the issues will appeal to all ability levels, the scripts will be found simple to read, with straightforward vocabulary. Similarly, the other writing in the volume has been kept at the same straightforward level.

A classroom reading, or semi-dramatisation, will obviously be the normal approach, but the scripts are especially effective also when recorded on tape. (I have contributed an account of producing sound radio plays in schools to the anthology *Worth a Hearing*, edited by Alfred Bradley, Blackie's *Student Drama Series*.) Indeed most of them will also *stage* very well, requiring only the minimum of furniture and an open stage. (*Last Bus* is the obvious exception to this.)

191

Inevitably the end of each play leads on to discussion—and a few "Talking points" have been provided to help group work and class talk (page 182). Many teachers will want to link further reading, writing, and in some cases research to the plays. I have included (p. 189) a short list of titles that would be suitable starters for further reading for pupils working on these scripts.

Finally, the many teachers anxious to discuss television as an art and communication media will find these a useful addition to the limited reprints of television plays available to school (a list is included on page 190). For this reason the producer of the series, Ronald Smedley, has written the explanatory description on page 162. This, however, does more than explain "how it is done"; it also sets readers thinking about the dramatic and artistic issues involved.

I should like to add a word of thanks to the various collaborators on the series. Ronald Eyre, who first showed that schools drama on television had a scope beyond the "classics"; Michael Simpson, who continued and expanded the work; and Ronald Smedley, who produced most of the plays in this book, including the now internationally famous one, *Last Bus*, which won the senior international award for educational television, the Japan Prize, in 1968.

MICHAEL MARLAND